UPROOTING
THE SINS OF
THE PAST

# Not Destroyed

**ARROW PRESS**

REBECCA HOLTZCLAW

Copyright © 2024 Rebecca Holtzclaw

All rights reserved. No part of this publication may be reproduced, distributed, or transmitted in any form or by any means, including photocopying, recording, or other electronic or mechanical methods, without the prior written permission of the publisher, except in the case of brief quotations embodied in critical reviews and certain other noncommercial uses permitted by copyright law. For permission requests, write to the publisher, addressed "Attention: Permissions Coordinator," at the address below.

Paperback: 978-1-951475-33-8
Ebook: 978-1-951475-34-5

Library of Congress Control Number: 2024906899

First paperback edition: June 2024

References to people, places, and events are based on the best recollection of the author and are not necessarily the thoughts or viewpoints of the publisher.

Arrow Press Publishing
Summerville, SC 29486

www.arrowpresspublishing.com

# Contents

An Altar Of Remembrance     7

CHAPTER 1: Breaking Up The Darkness     11
CHAPTER 2: A Small-Town Girl     17
CHAPTER 3: My Lonely World     29
CHAPTER 4: What's The Purpose Of All This?     37
CHAPTER 5: Into The Wilderness     41
CHAPTER 6: Major Life Changes     49
CHAPTER 7: I'm Not Who I Used To Be     57
CHAPTER 8: Out With The Old     63
CHAPTER 9: Forgiveness     71
CHAPTER 10: Revisiting The Past But Not Living In It     77
CHAPTER 11: Rooted     85
CHAPTER 12: Repentance Brings Restoration     91
CHAPTER 13: Out Of The Wilderness     97
CHAPTER 14: Obedience Brings Fire     103
CHAPTER 15: A New Life     111

APPENDIX: The Effects Of Childhood Abuse     115

# Acknowledgements

To my husband Kris who has supported me in so many areas of my life and has helped me with facing the fears that come with starting something new. One thing he shared with me years ago was that saying "If the turtle never stuck his head out of the shell he couldn't move forward (he wouldn't know what it was like out there)." His support continued while I poured my heart out on paper.

To my daughter Faith, one of the greatest gifts God has ever given me! God has made you strong, smart, beautiful and with purpose! I love you so much!!

To a very special friend Jessie who is like a younger sister to me. God has given her wisdom from a young age and she has given me wisdom throughout our friendship. She has listened to me share my heart, she has spoken the truth, prayed many times for me, my family, and she has been there when God has moved in powerful ways! From our serious God moments to our corny dad jokes, she is a huge blessing to me!! I love you friend!!

To my mom, family, and friends who have loved me in all stages of my life and for those who have prayed for me in all areas of my life!

To Sarah with By The By Editing helped me with my first line edit that helped me be prepared for the next step.

To Tim Twigg and his team at Arrow Publishing who gave me the detailed guidance that I needed to make this book a reality. They were professional, honest, and they stretched me in my writing process and captured my vision. I am so thankful for all they have done to make this book the best it can be.

NOT DESTROYED

# An Altar of Remembrance

*Shake off your dust; rise up, sit enthroned, Jerusalem. Free yourself from the chains on your neck, Daughter Zion, now a captive.*

ISAIAH 52:2 NIV

Not long after I got serious about writing this book, a thought popped into my head: *What makes my life so special that I need to write a book about it?*

It was a fair question. I'm not famous. I didn't invent anything. I'm just a girl from a small town who doesn't have the most desirable past. That almost makes it sound like I'm about to bust out singing "Don't Stop Believing'" by Journey. To be honest, though, that's exactly how I felt—I was a small-town girl, and I was growing up in a lonely world. But as I pondered the question of what makes my life special enough that I should write a book, an answer came to me.

*Nothing—yet everything.*

I wasn't sure what that meant, but I expected that by the end of the writing process, the answer would be more clear. It is—infinitely.

My life hasn't been easy. I know, nobody's has and some people have experienced worse things than I have. But I do believe I've had to overcome things that many people have never had to deal with, primarily childhood sexual abuse that affected every other aspect of my life. Perhaps this is your story too. If it is, I'm sorry. You've experienced something no child, or any person for that matter, should ever have to endure.

My childhood sexual abuse ended when I was eleven, but the ramifications tainted my life for many years, manifesting as low self-esteem, fear, worry, confusion, anxiety, doubt, and feeling unloved, unworthy, and stained. In addition to it affecting my relationships with people, it also affected my relationship with God. Children who have an unhealthy relationship with their earthly father (or father figure) often project that fathering experience onto their heavenly Father and struggle in their relationship with God. That was certainly my experience. While I knew about God from an early age, forming a relationship with Him took me years—and a lot of wandering.

Looking back now, I see my walk with God has been a lot like the Israelites' circling trek through the wilderness in Exodus 16–40. Just as they continually vacillated between trusting God fully to trusting in just about everything else but God, so did I. Just as they forgot all that God had done for them, so did I. And just like they finally stepped out of the wilderness and into their promised land, so did I, when I finally surrendered everything to God.

No, my life hasn't been easy. I've experienced a lot of evil because of other's sins. Even so, I wasn't destroyed. God has loved me fiercely, even when I didn't realize it. He has been patient with me as I struggled with my past and how it affected my actions and reactions in the present. And He has brought healing and hope that I once thought impossible. He did it for me, and I know He can do it for you as well.

Another thing the Israelites did was set up altars to remember times when they saw God's faithfulness to them (see Exodus 17:15; 24:4; Joshua 8:30; 24:25–27). They did this in remembrance of what the Lord had done for them so they and others, namely their children, wouldn't forget His faithfulness (see Joshua 4:6–7). For me, this book is a type of altar of remembrance. Writing it has allowed me to look back on my life and see God's faithfulness over and over, and once it's published and in hand, it will be a physical reminder for me—and anyone who reads it—that our Lord "is able to do immeasurably more than all we ask or imagine, according to his power that is at work within us" (Ephesians 3:20 NIV).

In my journey of writing this book and going back and forth with the edits, I found myself in a place of digging deeper and allowing God to pull more things out of me. I didn't realize that I still had some past things hidden away. There were some things that I'd just brushed aside and never called them what they were. I also had to finally have a difficult but necessary conversation with my mom.

It was hard to follow through with what God was showing me. To share more detail of my abuse and the feelings that elicited brought up some emotional rebellion. I didn't want to do it! I wanted to be superficial, just stay on the surface level, but that's not what I want for me or for my readers. I don't want you to stay on the surface level of your past, your hurts, your pain, and the hidden areas of your life. By digging deeper, you will get emotional and probably cry, I promise you that. But the healing that comes is so worth it! Allowing God to uproot the sins of the past will allow the healing He longs to give you (see Psalm 147:3).

That's why I share my life in a vulnerable way—with the hope that it'll speak to you and compel you to surrender to God and allow His healing light to banish any darkness of the past in your life. When you finish this book, I pray you'll walk away feeling free, having a new understanding of yourself, having a sense of purpose, and being open to forgiving, renewing your mind with a fresh perspective, and knowing that you are loved and accepted by God (see Ephesians 1:4).

## CHAPTER 1

# Breaking up the Darkness

*Do not gloat over me, my enemy! Though I have fallen, I will rise. Though I sit in the darkness, the LORD will be my light.*

MICAH 7:8 NIV

Have you ever thought that when you got your life together, when your spouse got their life together, and when your kids were doing well, that would be when God could really use you? That's how I felt for a long time. For the last few years, God has been calling me and guiding me in a new direction. Even with this guidance, though, I kept thinking the time to move forward with getting serious about being bold for God wasn't right because my life wasn't perfect. I wasn't perfect, and I still had struggles to deal with, so I questioned whether God could really use me in the ways I felt He was leading me. "Who am I, God?" I asked. But I greatly desired more of what He wanted for my life.

Through the years, I felt like every time I'd draw near to God—when He'd show me more of how He wanted to use me and who I was to Him and I'd feel His presence—something would happen and I'd get sidetracked and be filled with doubt and insecurities, which led me to become stuck in my own head. For years that was my cycle, and it made me feel like I'd wasted so much time.

Then, a few years ago, I read a book called *It's Not Supposed to Be This Way* by Lysa TerKeurst and it really opened my eyes. She wrote this book during an incredibly difficult time in her life, and I had to wonder how she could write in the middle of such pain. Her story showed me that even in that challenging time, her words and her faith went beyond the pain and turned her toward Jesus. She remained faithful to writing the book, allowing God to work through her so His bigger purpose would be fulfilled. She didn't say, "This is what I'm going through right now. God can't use me. I have to get fixed first." If we all did that—waited until everything in our life was "fixed"—we would never do anything. Life brings the unexpected all the time.

After that, one Sunday at church the pastor talked about knowing our history, our family's history, our spouse's history, and God's Word. By knowing this history, we can see what God has done in our own life and in others' lives. We're able to see the miracle that happened, and that fills us with hope and joy by showing us the grace, power, and glory of God.

As I considered Lysa's ability to write during such a turbulent time, I thought about my own history. Many times I'd tried to write out the things I experienced while growing up, but my emotions would get in the way. I wouldn't get far, and eventually I'd stop writing. Despite how I'd avoid going back to it, God kept nudging me to finish what I'd started. The problem with facing our past, our fears, and our hurts is we also have to face the pain they still bring. It was a process I had to commit to.

This process made me think of a tattoo my aunt got in her early twenties. The tattoo artist didn't do a very good job and she never liked it. Later, she had another artist try to tattoo over it, but that didn't look good either. For years she lived with this thing—something she didn't like from the moment it was complete—on her skin. She tried to keep it covered, and years later she had the dark, unrecognizable tattoo removed.

My thoughts about this led me to do some research on tattoo removal. I found it interesting that the human body typically removes foreign particles by means of the immune system, but ink particles are too large. Also, because the ink is below the skin's surface, removing it is more complex.

Tattoo removal can be done in a few ways. One popular choice is laser treatments. The laser—a focused beam of light—heats up the ink to break it into smaller particles that the immune system can then remove. These treatments are painful (often more so than the actual tattoo), require multiple sessions, and can cause some scarring. As well, after each treatment, the area needs to heal before another treatment can be done.

It seems to me that facing our past and the things that have left a permanent mark on us is similar. First, we have to decide to face whatever left that permanent mark. Then, after accepting the pain that might be involved, we have to get laser focused on removing what doesn't belong.

I have to think that if my aunt had removed the first tattoo instead of trying to cover it up, the removal wouldn't have required so many treatments or been so painful. With two tattoos, there was a lot of dark ink there—just like the dark things that have happened in our lives. And when we try to cover these things with other dark things, eventually we can't stand the ugliness and have to face them.

That hurts! It takes time to remove permanent marks that have been left on us. But with each session, we allow the beam of light to break up the darkness and heal us little by little. And once we heal from one painful thing, we can persevere and break up the next thing.

The darkness from my abuse had me reaching for the goal of perfection as if it would cover up what had been done to me in my childhood. But the stains of my past remained with a feeling of shame.

I now have learned that I don't have to get everything perfect for God to meet me right where I am. I just need to be willing to sit at the feet of Jesus and allow His light to penetrate every dark area in my life. Even though we are sinners, God sent Jesus to die for us (Romans 5:8). Christ died for the ungodly. God didn't say, "Get your life together first and then I will work in and through you." He said, "Come to me, all you who are weary" (Matthew 11:28), "Believe me and understand that I am [God]" (Isaiah 43:10), "I love those who love me, and those who search for me find me" (Proverbs 8:17), "My grace is sufficient for you, for my power is perfected in weakness" (2 Corinthians 12:9), and "Do not fear, for I am with you; do not be afraid, for I am your God. I will strengthen you; I will help you" (Isaiah 41:10).

The pain of my past was real. The physical, sexual, and mental abuse was real. It couldn't be just covered up and forgot about. I needed God to meet me in my pain—in my imperfection. I had to face my past and the legitimacy of the effects from my abuse.

> **I needed God to meet me in my pain— in my imperfection**

In the appendix of this book I have included statistics and information on the effects of child abuse. The information was helpful to me to understand how my abuse affected me, and learning about it has helped me understand my struggles and to make changes. I've also learned that there are resources to help with recovery and healing. Just because a person has been a victim of abuse doesn't mean they have to stay a victim throughout their life. Proverbs 23:7(KJV) says; "As he thinketh in his heart, so is he." I needed a new way to "thinketh." I needed a "new heart"—a renewal of my mind.

# CHAPTER 2

# A Small-Town Girl

*Though my father and mother forsake me,
the Lord will receive me.*

**PSALM 27:10 NIV**

Way, way back in the 1900s—May of 1978 to be exact—my mother was dropped off at a hospital in Caribou, Maine, to give birth by herself. She was divorced—a single mom who was already raising one daughter. The child she was about to give birth to was, in her eyes, fatherless.

Sometimes I wonder what went through her mind that day. I wonder if she thought, *Did I make the right decision—to have this child?* I know she had a conversation about abortion with the father. But that day—no doubt scared, confused, and in pain—my mother gave birth to a little girl. Me.

> **For you created my inmost being; you knit me together in my mother's womb.**
> **PSALM 139:13 NIV**

In writing this book, as I pondered memories from my childhood, I had a hard time remembering the age I was when some of them happened. Some of my memories are fractured because of the things I blocked out. To get an idea of my age, I often went by the places where I lived at the time to determine about how old I was.

When I think of my childhood, I don't automatically get a happy feeling or remember a sweet memory. I certainly have good memories, but the bad ones can easily overshadow them. I think that happens with a lot of things in life. For example, we can hold on to hurtful things said or done by people we're close to—like our spouse, our parents, or our children—and forget about their good qualities or the nice things they've said to us. Even now as I sit here writing this, my mind wants to ruminate on the not-so-good memories instead of the happy ones.

Throughout my childhood, I hid a lot of what was going on at home. I didn't want anyone to know about it. And I was afraid. I was afraid I'd get in trouble, I'd be looked at differently, or people would think it was my fault. There was also the fear that if I told someone, that would confirm it was real, and I didn't know how that would shape my life. I felt so much shame. I was afraid of what people would think about my mom staying with a husband who was abusive. I wanted to protect her from blame. I didn't want her to be hurt.

What was going on at home took place at the hands of a man I'll call Mr. M, who was my mom's second husband. Mom started dating Mr. M when I was around two years old, and they got divorced when I was eleven, so he was in my life during crucial periods of my growth and development. I honestly can't say exactly when the abuse started. I don't remember, but I can tell you how I felt growing up—timid, shameful, broken, nervous, and fearful.

We lived in an apartment complex in Presque Isle that had been built in 1944. The buildings were in bad shape when we lived there in the late 1970s, and a few years later they ended up being condemned. In 1984, they were burned down by the local fire department. I have few memories of that apartment because I was so young. According to my mom, I lived there from birth to age three. I find that a little surprising since I remember the layout of the apartment and getting a bath in the kitchen sink.

When you walked into the apartment, there was a refrigerator to the left and a table next to it. To the right were the counters and sink. Straight ahead was the living room, which always seemed so dark. I remember the pull string for the light in the bedroom, or maybe it was the bathroom. I also recall that in the winter Mom would close off part of the apartment because the rooms were so cold, there'd be frost on the walls. She told me that during the winter, she, my sister Jen, and I would all sleep on the pull-out couch in the living room to stay warm.

The next place we lived was a low-income apartment in a complex that had just been built. I was so happy when we moved there. It was a new neighborhood with a playground right next to our apartment. My friend Karen moved in a street over from us, and my other friend, Dannielle, moved into the apartments just across the road. It was so nice to live in a building that'd just been built. Everything was new, with fresh paint, no scratches, and no holes on the walls. Our apartment seemed large at the time. It had a basement, and Jen and I had our own rooms, which was exciting for us.

Jen is three years older than me. When we were young, I felt like it was her and me, and then there was the rest of the world. I considered her the strong one. We would argue at times, but we were very close. She could mess with me, but she would not let anyone else do that.

Sometimes I'd get made fun of in school and wouldn't stick up for myself. I was taller than average, and in fourth and fifth grade my body was changing rapidly. Looking back, I realize I wasn't overweight, but I felt like I was because I was taller and bigger than most of the other kids. One day, a boy told me he would date me if I'd lose some weight. I laugh about it now because he was probably half my height—and I can think of some great comebacks—but at the time I was crushed.

I told Jen about some of the girls who were harassing me, and she showed me what I needed to do if they tried to fight me. She taught me some moves to protect myself, moves that would take them down to the ground. And she showed me how to make a fist and explained to not tuck my thumb inside my fist because I could hurt my thumb that way.

When I was at school, I'd keep in mind what I'd need to do if they came at me. Jen was a few years ahead of me, so when I was in fourth and fifth grade she was in middle school. If we'd been in the same school, she would've made sure those girls didn't give me any trouble.

At home, my sister and I would listen to Mom and Mr. M fight in their bedroom. We knew it got physical sometimes because of the sounds. And he'd also been physical with us. We knew how he was. Jen remembers seeing marks on our mom after their fights.

One day when I was maybe six years old, I was spending some time with my mom in her room, sitting on the end of her bed talking to her while she was putting clothes away or something like that. Mr. M walked into the room and smacked me in the mouth, then walked out. I could taste blood, and when I put my hand up to my mouth it was bleeding.

Mom got upset and we left the apartment to go out for a ride. That was what she'd always do when they'd get into a fight. We had a black station wagon that she'd fold down the back of so Jen and I could sleep when it was late. We thought that was fun, lying in the back of the car, not buckled into our seats. Plus, we liked it when she left so we'd all be away from him. The night he made my mouth bleed, when we went back to the apartment, he had me sit on his knee in the kitchen and apologized for hitting me. That was the first time I'd ever heard him apologize for hitting one of us.

Jen and I can now laugh about some things to make light of what we experienced. For example, we talk about when we'd race up the stairs to the second floor of the apartment, trying to be the first one up when Mr. M was coming after us. We knew the slowest one would be the one who'd get their butt kicked. So I tried to be faster, but she was older and stronger. Sometimes I would get ahead of her, though, and she'd get the brunt of it.

Even though we fought like sisters do, I would talk to Jen about a lot of things. She and I were both physically and mentally abused by Mr. M, but I was the only one who was sexually abused. When I was in maybe third grade, Jen said something about boys, and I told her about what a male babysitter had done to me a few years before (I barely remember what happened now or what I said to her, but I still remember the room where the abuse happened.) She told me I'd been molested, but I didn't even know what that word meant. Jen then went to Mom and told her, and she was very upset. She knew which babysitter had done it by the detail of the room I'd described.

I was afraid because I'd never told anyone about what Mr. M had been doing to me. I didn't know how he'd react at hearing about someone else doing the same thing. Mr. M seemed like he was so upset that someone had done that to me. Now I know he was just playing the part.

Time went by, and I continued to remain silent about what was happening in our home. Then one day when I was maybe ten years old, I told my sister about "wrestling" with Mr. M. I don't remember exactly what I said, but it had to do with me feeling uncomfortable. I was trying to tell her without actually telling her. I just couldn't say it! How do you just come out and say it? I was afraid.

So Jen said something to our mom. Mom talked with me, and I'm sure I lied and made light of it. I didn't want to seem like I was telling on him. In the end, she said he was just playing, so I left it at that. Later, when my sister and I were alone in the car, she told me, "If he ever does something, you tell me." But I never did tell her.

Mr. M was always pretty strict. He wanted the house clean, our beds made, and dishes rinsed before being put in the sink. He insisted that things be done a certain way (his dad had been in the military and was the same way), and I can't say those things were bad, but it was the fear he caused that made me try to do everything perfectly. He also had other rules, like Jen and I only being able to buy candy and watch movies on the weekends, which continued until I was maybe in second or third grade. He also didn't accept mistakes. One night at dinner I accidentally put ketchup on my corn, and he made me sit at the table until I ate it all. (I sat there for a long time that night.) He didn't care that I'd made a mistake; he wasn't going to let me waste anything. I found out years later that Mr. M's mother was very strict and had a temper, and she raised him and his brothers with very high expectations of them.

One night, I woke up to him yelling at me because I wasn't wearing the proper clothes to bed. I had on the sweater I'd worn that day, and I'd been cold, so I didn't want to take it off to change. It was wintertime and very cold in northern Maine. I still don't know why he was in my room and knew what I was wearing, but he was always checking on me.

I have other memories from different times in my childhood of waking up in the middle of the night with him there in my bedroom and my mom coming in and arguing with him because he was mad about something. Other times it was just him. Going to bed at night was always scary because I was afraid there might be something under my bed or that something was going to get me. I'd tell myself I wasn't scared and keep my eyes closed. Sometimes, I'd take all my stuffed animals and surround my body with them as if they'd protect me. As much as I wanted to run to my mom to feel safe, I knew I'd get in trouble. Besides, Mr. M was in her bedroom with her. I desperately wanted to be held and comforted, but I told myself I needed to get over my fears and go to sleep.

I was a deep sleeper (when I did sleep), and I believe abuse happened while I slept. There would be times when I'd wake up and Mr. M would be in my room. A few years ago, I asked Jen what she remembered from our childhood, and she described many of the same details I remembered. In fact, she recalled more than I did. I now understand that's because I blocked out and detached from many of the experiences. It's crazy how abuse can mess with your mind. You learn to block stuff out, deal with things you should never have to deal with, and justify the abuse—all of which follows you throughout your whole life.

By the time I was eleven and Jen was fourteen, we had moved two more times. The street we lived on now had some big, beautiful homes on it. I'd roller skate and ride my bike and wonder what the people who lived in those homes were like. My sister used to pet-sit for our neighbor across the street, and one time I went with her to help. The house smelled nice when we walked in, and I thought it was so cool that they had a garage. I think she really liked pet sitting for them because she wanted to be out of the house.

This was about the time Jen started acting out and rebelling. She'd had enough and she didn't want to be controlled anymore. She ran off to a friend's house one day, and Mr. M and Mom couldn't find her. She didn't want to come home; she wanted Mr. M gone. The next time she ran off and was then brought back home, it turned into a big fight.

We were in the kitchen, and my mom, Jen, and I had all had enough of Mr. M's treatment of us. Jen no longer wanted to live at home if he was living there. During this fight, Mr. M raised his hand to hit my sister and Mom stepped in the way and told him to leave. That was the last time he had a chance to lay his hand on any of us. My mom wasn't backing down this time, and Jen stood firm in her decision to leave if he didn't. But even though Mr. M left and no longer had physical control of us, he still had a mental hold due to the trauma he caused.

Not long before this fallout I found out with certainty that Mr. M wasn't my biological father, even though deep down I'd known he wasn't. (Later I learned that since I was so young when Mom and Mr. M met, they just told me he was my dad.) When I was upset at Mr. M, Jen would tell me he wasn't really our dad. I'd also had a conversation with Mr. M's parents that I'd never shared with anyone. When I was riding in the car with them one day, they'd said they'd be my grandparents if I wanted them to be. I believe that's how I knew all those years that Mr. M wasn't my dad. I didn't dare say anything to Mom or Mr. M, but I wondered who my dad actually was. I had so many questions that I didn't ask.

My mom had been married to my sister's father, so Jen knew who her dad was. He was also in her life some. When it came out that Mr. M wasn't my dad, Mom finally gave me some details about my biological father. She didn't know much about him, just that he was going to the college in our small town when they met.

I'd always felt like Mom held things back and kept a lot of secrets. But I didn't ask many questions either. She could be sensitive, and I didn't like to upset her. I wasn't afraid of my mom (she wasn't the one physically abusing us), but I didn't want to take on her emotions along with mine. I knew these questions might bring up emotions in her that she may not want to deal with and I didn't want to either. Many times when I'd go through her pictures, I'd look for photos of men and wonder if any of them were my dad. I did this even before I found out for sure about Mr. M. I just wanted to know what my dad looked like. My mom was blond with blue eyes, and I don't look like her, so as I looked through pictures I wondered if I would recognize a face similar to mine. Though I felt abandoned and believed my father didn't want me, I wanted to see his face.

Mom and Mr. M got divorced, and once he left our home he never abused me again. The messed-up thing is that I stayed in contact with him till I graduated from high school. He was the only dad I'd ever known. Even though he was abusive, he also taught me how to read and helped me with my homework. I was always scared he'd yell at me if I messed up, but I also longed for his approval when I did well. He was an artist, and I loved art and learned some things from him.

So I blocked out all he'd done and still talked to him. He even came to my high school graduation. When I think about that now, it seems so crazy. For years I continued this pattern, allowing things in my life that weren't healthy.

The year of my graduation, I wrote a letter to Mr. M's parents because I cared about them. They'd been very good to me when my mom was married to Mr. M, but after the divorce they didn't stay in touch. I wasn't their biological grandchild, but I still felt abandoned by them. I didn't give full details in the letter, knowing they thought the divorce was all my mom's fault, but I let them know about some of the things Mr. M had done.

I was so hurt because I felt like they'd loved me but then let me go like I wasn't important. I have happy memories with them. They would buy me things, take me places, and get me special snacks to eat that I wouldn't get at home. I felt so spoiled—and I felt safe with them. The year of my graduation, and after writing that letter to Mr. M's parents, was when I shut the door on that part of my life and moved on. I had nothing more to do with Mr. M or his family.

I've always wondered why, with abuse, people don't speak up and tell someone what's going on until many years later. But I didn't speak up. I never told a teacher, never told another family member, never told the authorities. Even after one of my childhood friend's abuse by her father was exposed and she went to court, I kept my abuse to myself. She spoke up about it, but I still couldn't.

I'm thankful Mr. M never sexually abused my sister, but Jen has held on to a lot of guilt, thinking that it was her job to protect me but she wasn't able to. It saddens me to know she feels like she'd failed to protect me, because that was never her job. I've told her that if she hadn't spoken out and left home, the abuse would've went on for longer. Because of her it pushed Mom to make the choice to make Mr. M leave. I'm thankful for my sister's strength to speak up and not back down.

It was only after I moved away from Maine to South Carolina, at the age of thirty-one, that I was able to fully admit what happened and even say the word abuse when talking about my childhood. Some close friends during my childhood found out that abuse happened in my home, but I never wanted to talk about it or give any details. While I never shared in complete detail even after I moved to South Carolina, I felt like I could talk about bits and pieces and admit that I'd been abused. Being in a new area many states away from my hometown, where no one knew my mom, my family, or my abusers, gave me the freedom and security to share without worrying that what I said would get back to them.

While writing this book, I realized that I've actually shared more this year than I have during the rest of my life as a whole. Until recently, even some of my close friends didn't know what my childhood had been like. And some won't know until they read this book.

It took me a long time to accept the details of my past—to say it out loud and to type it here in this book, and this is just a small part of it. This writing process has opened up more areas that I needed to release, and it's been healing for me. God has shown me the importance of sharing my story—my testimony.

A couple of weeks ago, I was reading the apostle Paul's testimony in Acts 9. Before Paul's encounter with Christ, he was named Saul and his priority was murdering followers of Jesus Christ. He had an experience with Jesus that was so powerful, it brought him to his knees and blinded him. Afterward, being filled with the Holy Spirt and having regained his sight, he changed his life completely. He wasn't superficial about his testimony and instead put all his strength into living with purpose and boldness for the Lord. He was a changed man with a new name.

Later, when being persecuted, Paul pleaded his case in front of top officials and anyone who was in earshot heard about his journey on the way to Damascus where God met him and changed him. Some accepted his

> **He didn't just say, "I had an experience."**

testimony and some did not, but Paul continued to serve the Lord even during times of suffering. He didn't just say, "I had an experience." He described it in detail. I love that Paul's details are not focused on his past, but on his experience with Christ. When I think about my own story, I'm quick to share about the day I fell on my knees and cried out to God, and all that He has done since then.

God is in the details of our life. He was in the details of mine and He is in the details of yours. Like Paul's, our testimony can encourage change in others. If we seek God, He meets us right where we are in a powerful way. My past does not define me, and your past doesn't define you. And the difficult things we've experienced can become what give us our greatest purpose.

## CHAPTER 3

# My Lonely World

*Nothing in all creation is hidden form God's sight. Everything is uncovered and laid bare before the eyes of him to whom we must give account.*

**HEBREWS 4:13 NIV**

The good thing was that Jen, my mom, and I didn't have to live in that abuse anymore. Mr. M was out of our lives and we were no longer under his control. My sister, who was in high school, took advantage of her new freedom and started partying.

I, in middle school, went through a dark phase that included watching every scary movie I could. I also made a Ouija board with a friend and would ask the board so many questions, including who my biological father was. (I always wondered if it was my friend who was moving the planchette around the board, though it never gave good answers anyway.) My mind seemed to believe life was better in my dreams while I slept because my reality was riddled with confusion, depression, and feeling so lost.

I was around thirteen when I finally felt relatively comfortable talking to my mom about what had happened to me as a child, but it wasn't a straight-forward admission. With her I couldn't just describe the details. It was my sister who told Mom about the sexual abuse after she read my diary. That's when Mom asked if something had happened to me.

When she asked, I felt so mad. I remember saying yes, then thinking, *Like, really? You're going to ask me that now? Two years after this man is out of our lives.* We never discussed the details of what Mr. M had done, and she told me not to tell the family because they would blame her.

I was hurt by her response, but I did keep it to myself. I wanted to protect her even though I didn't feel protected. There were so many secrets and unsaid things. Now I understand how that had been an unspoken rule in my family for generations. It was just what we did. We didn't talk about it. We didn't get help. We kept everything a secret. Yes, my mom had made mistakes throughout her life, but she also faced things that she'd kept to herself and was told to keep secret. I don't think she wanted anyone to know about the family dysfunction. She was great at blocking things out as if they never happened as well—and if blocking things out could be genetic, it definitely passed down to me.

I did finally talk with my mom about these feelings I had, but it wasn't till I was in the process of writing this book. I still held back from telling her how I truly felt. I have forgiven her, so I didn't think telling her these things was what I needed to do, but that was my idea, not what God was pressing me toward. For years He'd reminded me to have that conversation with her, but I was like "I'm good." God knows better, though, and there was more healing that needed to take place in me and my mom. I now wish I had had that conversation sooner.

By high school I'd left that dark phase behind, but I acted out in other ways. I drank alcohol for the first time when I was fourteen, and throughout high school I drank and partied. I also dated guys who weren't good for me. Some were too old to be dating a high schooler, and some took advantage of me physically or wanted to control me. Because of my childhood, I thought control and abuse were normal in a relationship, and even that their desire for control meant they loved me. I wanted to feel loved and protected, but I was attracted to the wrong kind of guy.

During that time, there were many nights when I'd black out from drinking. One night I remember being drunk and I was so tired and passed out in my bed with my older boyfriend who I had already been intimate with in the past, so I knew when I woke up the next day, my body felt different, like we'd had sex. But I didn't remember anything happening after I'd gone to bed the night before. I said something to him about how I was feeling, and he got defensive, turned it around on me, and got mad at me for not remembering us having sex. I was confused why he would have sex with me while I was passed out, someone who I trusted and thought loved me. I never brought up what happened the night again. Because of what happened that night, I layered more blame and shame onto myself. That boyfriend ended up being unfaithful and physically abusive.

I want to add here that this was extremely difficult to write. I wanted to delete it many times. Then I prayed about sharing this and realized that some readers may have experienced something similar and may have put the blame and shame on themselves. If that's the case for you, I'm telling you that it should have never happened to you and it's not your fault. Don't believe that lie. Roman's 12:21 tells us not to let evil defeat us.

After this boyfriend and I broke up, I woke up at my mother's house one morning to find his one hand over my mouth and the other around my neck. He said, "I just wanted to put the fear in you," then let go of me and left. I called my mom and Jen, neither of whom were home, and one of them called the police but both of them made it to the house before the police did.

I was so thankful the state pressed charges even when I chose not to due to fear, and was thankful for the restraining order enacted against him, but what my ex-boyfriend did kept me on edge for a long time. Who knows what would've happened if I hadn't called the police and he would've had legal access to me. I did have to face him in court, although I now barely remember it because it's something I chose to stop thinking about a long time ago.

Despite the difficult environment of my childhood, I did receive some religious training. When I was young, Mom would sometimes send me to Sunday school, where I'd learn about some of the children's Bible stories. She believed in God and told me we were Christians, and her mother had been raised in a Christian home and was strong in her faith. I believed in God even though I didn't know much about Him, and I prayed to Him and believed He was watching over me.

When I was young, I had a plaque that hung on the wall next to my bed. On it a little boy and a little girl were walking across a broken bridge with an angel behind them, watching over them. The inscription read, "Angel of God, my guardian dear, to whom God's love commits me here, ever this day be at my side, to light and guard, to rule and guide. Amen." Many nights I'd lay in bed looking at it because it gave me some peace. (When my daughter was little, I hung it on her bedroom wall, and it's now on my bookshelf.)

When I went to a Christian camp in my teens, I asked Jesus into my heart. I loved being at camp and made some good friends there, but I was still feeling lost inside and making bad choices. God was with me, though. There would be times when I'd be out drinking at a "pit party" (a party in the woods or a field), and I'd go off by myself and cry out to God—you know, the "Why me, God?" prayers. I spent many drunken nights crying in a field. I tried filling the emptiness inside me with all the wrong things.

I felt unloved, stupid, and ugly, and I struggled under the weight of shame and the idea that I wasn't good enough. Since I tried to hide that from people, I cried out to God, even though I didn't fully understand who He was. There was so much I didn't understand—Him, the Bible, my own life. But I knew I was searching for something.

As I got older, I became very independent. In high school I worked, went to school, and got good grades even though I partied. I wanted to prove to myself that I could do well in school and that I didn't need anyone. I struggled academically but would work hard and get my work done. I actually ended up being on the honor roll my last two years of high school.

At this point, my mother was focused on herself, my new stepdad, and Jen, who was dealing with her own life challenges. I felt so alone but would never admit it. I didn't want anyone to see my weaknesses. I wouldn't voice that I needed anyone, and I believed that I didn't.

My new stepdad was the man my mom married after divorcing Mr. M. She'd been with him since I was eleven. For the longest time, I didn't see him as a father but as someone who was always there for me if I needed anything. He was a good man—and still is—but at the time he came into my life, and after everything that'd happened, I didn't want a father. So I just did my own thing. Independence is funny. It's a good thing, and yet taken to the extreme it can make you hard inside, and that's what I was. After fighting so many inner battles on my own, I saw nothing wrong with continuing to fight alone.

The summer after I graduated from high school, I moved down near Bar Harbor, Maine, to work and live with my aunt and uncle. To this day, the

Bar Harbor area is one of my favorite places. I loved living there, and my aunt and uncle were—and always have been—so good to me. They believed in me, even when my life was a mess.

I got homesick fairly quickly, though, and moved back to Presque Isle and decided to go to college. I also started dating someone I'd gone to high school with. Then when I was twenty I got pregnant with my daughter, Faith. I married her father after she was born, but it wasn't a good relationship. I knew I shouldn't marry him, but he was the father of my child, and I was sure he'd never let me be with someone else. So I married him. He was very controlling and manipulating, and sometimes physically abusive. I thought I loved him, and since I'd known abuse my whole life, I thought it was normal in a relationship.

While I was in the hospital waiting to give birth to Faith (the doctor was going to induce me the next morning), Faith's dad went to get me some food and then took off to go hang out with friends. I was alone when my water broke. Some family and friends showed up then, but my boyfriend didn't return for maybe an hour after. He was there before the birth of our beautiful daughter, though.

Our relationship was hard. He spent most of his time at his friends' houses playing video games. When Faith was an infant, I'd have to call around to see which house he was at. I felt so stupid doing that, and sometimes I'd just go to bed wondering when he'd come home. Many nights I'd hold Faith and cry, though I never shared this with anyone. I didn't want people to think something was wrong with me or that I was depressed. With him I acted like I didn't need anything, because when I expected or hoped for something, he wouldn't come through. Handling as much as I could on my own was how I protected myself from being let down. Instead, I focused on my daughter and what she needed. I wanted to make sure she felt loved and would never have to deal with the same feelings I did while growing up.

When Faith's dad gave me a ring and asked me to marry him, I wasn't sure if I would follow through with it. But I kept moving forward in the relationship because I still thought I loved him, and that he loved me, but I struggled with how he treated me and wasn't there for me when he should have been. We didn't have much, but I did my best to make sure Faith never went without. When she was born, we lived in a subsidized apartment and our furniture had been donated to us. I was thankful for food stamps and WIC even though I felt embarrassed when using them at the store. I didn't want to need that type of help, but it was my only option—although I determined I wasn't going to stay in that situation.

When Faith was five months old, I decided to put college on hold and go to cosmetology school instead. So I went to school during the week and worked on the weekends. Faith spent most days with her dad or his aunt while I was in school or working. I finally graduated after a year of schooling and got a job in the hair industry. In time I moved out of subsidized housing, bought a new trailer, and had it placed in a small trailer park out in the country.

I worked hard to provide for us all. When Faith was two years old, her dad and I got married. Sometimes he would work, but most of the time he didn't. In addition to being abusive, he would steal money and other things from me. So many times I wondered if I was crazy—if it was just me. I would ask my close friends to be honest and tell me if there was something wrong with me and they would reassure me that I was not crazy.

He didn't like me having close friends or spending much time with other people. If I'd spend a lot of time with one of my girlfriends, he'd ask if I was a lesbian. I also had to let him know where I was at all times, and I wasn't allowed to talk about certain things in front of his friends. If I looked in the direction of another man, he'd say I must want him. If I talked to anyone, he'd start a fight. If I wanted to wear nice undergarments, he'd ask who I was wearing them for. When I finally got a cell phone, I had to always know exactly where I was so that if he called me, I could tell him. He would twist our conversations so I'd end up feeling bad for him, and he loved manipulating other people by doing the same thing. Our marriage felt like such darkness, and yet he would threaten me with saying things like he would take Faith if I ever left him. He would say things to make me feel worthless. Every day of our marriage was an emotional roller coaster with way more lows than highs.

One evening while doing laundry, I cried out to God, pleading for change—for my husband to change or for something to happen that would end the relationship. Two days later, my husband physically assaulted me again. It happened so fast. He came at me, and I ended up landing on the shoe rack on the floor of our closet. It broke and scraped down the side of my body, causing bruises all over me.

> ... this is not where God left me...

That was when I knew I'd had enough. I made him leave, and eventually we divorced. I had spent six years of my life with him. It was still hard afterward, though. He was still in my life because we had a child together, and I had a lot to heal and move forward from. The great thing is this is not where God left me—as a woman with a dark past and a failed marriage, a single mom just trying to survive.

Even despite our sin and corruption, Jesus still came to free us from the bondage of the results of sin (Romans 5:8). He came to take it all away (Hebrews 9:28). He loves us and wants us to experience that love, so much so that He gave himself up for us (Ephesians 5:2).

This reconciliation is available for all of us—the broken, the poor, the outcast. No matter our past, no matter our failures, Jesus came to give us freedom. He met the Samaritan woman right where she was at (John 4). He came to her knowing her past and her current situation, and He still offered her living water—salvation. He offers us the same. We only need to accept it.

## CHAPTER 4

# What's the Purpose of All This?

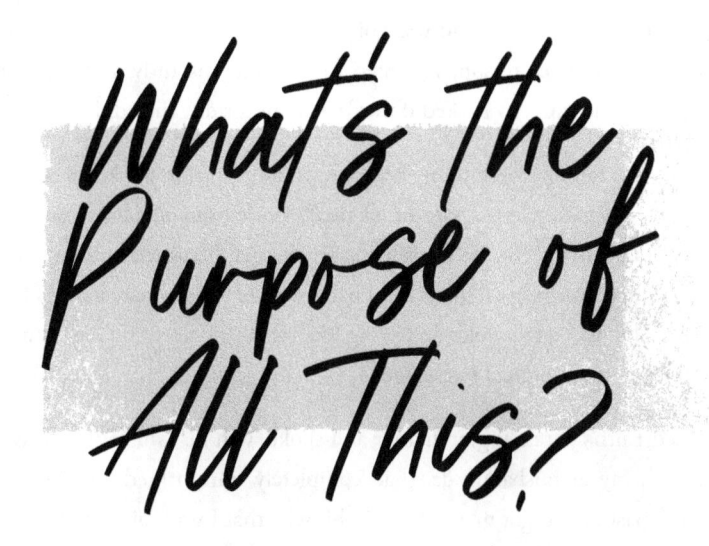

> *I make known the end from the beginning from ancient times, what is still to come. I say, "my purpose will stand, and I will do all that I please."*
>
> **ISAIAH 46:10 NIV**

I continued to work and be Faith's mom. If my daughter was at her grandparents' house over the weekend, I'd party—but never around her. I didn't want her exposed to anything like that. Partying on the weekends was fun in the moment, though, and it helped me escape my life and not have to think. Overwhelmed with trying to keep moving forward with all the stuff I was carrying from my past and keeping it together for my daughter, I wanted to numb my thoughts. I wanted to let loose and feel free from my responsibilities. That feeling was just for a short time, though. It never filled the emptiness I felt inside.

In 2006, I had an aha moment. I'd gotten off work, then went to a party down the road from where I lived. For some reason that night I didn't feel like drinking, so I didn't. Sitting there in a chair, in a stranger's apartment, I looked around and thought, *What's the purpose of all this?* I had the urge to go home, so I got up and was going to walk since I didn't live too far away. For whatever reason, I wanted to be home instantly. A couple of people were leaving, so I asked if they'd give me a ride. They did.

When I got home, I went to my bedroom and dropped to my knees beside my bed. "What's the purpose of all this?" I cried out to God. I simply couldn't take living the life I was living any longer. I crawled onto my bed and lay there weeping till it felt like I had no more tears to release and I fell asleep. The next day I woke up feeling like I'd fallen asleep in God's arms, knowing something had to change.

I called Faith's paternal grandfather and spoke with his wife. While I was married, my ex-husband's dad had completely transformed his life, become a pastor, and got married. I told his wife that I was going to change, although I didn't know what that meant yet. I just knew I was supposed to tell someone who might understand. She suggested I read *The Purpose Driven Life: What on Earth Am I Here For?* by Rick Warren.

Reading that book opened my eyes and altered my understanding. I realized there was so much about God that I didn't know (for example, I thought people who died became angels; I had no idea God created angels). As I learned about who God really is and His amazing love, my heart began to soften. I wanted more of Him.

For the first time in my life, I had such joy! I felt special and loved. The emptiness I'd struggled with was gone. I began to seek God, and I read His Word, went to church, and attended as many church functions as I could. I wanted to know more, and I had so many questions. It was like a whole new world opened up for me.

I began to change as a person. I forgave those who'd harmed me in the past and began to heal. I loved people in a new way. After all those years of pain, I felt like I was being held, finally experiencing that feeling I'd longed for as a child. I felt safe in God's arms.

I believe that the people we meet, the things we go through, and the things we learn along the way all can mold us in many ways and make us who we are—even the most difficult things, like my past marriage. It took my ex-husband and me to make my daughter, Faith. She's unique and perfectly created by God, and is the greatest gift He's ever given me aside from Jesus. My ex-husband's dad spoke a lot of truth into my life and even baptized me. Even though we don't have a relationship now, he played a big part in my life back then. My ex-husband's nana was another person in my life who loved God, answered my many questions, and encouraged my faith. She's now with Jesus, but I often think of her and the love she showed me. It amazes me how many people God put in my life to help me find Him.

I started counseling with a pastor at the church I was attending at the time. I had so many questions, like whether I could (biblically) remarry and what this new life meant for me with the past I had. My desire was to do whatever God wanted me to do. I was all-in! After some counseling, I chose to attend a class called Spiritual Cleansing with two pastors.

I wasn't worried, because I was ready, but I was a bit nervous. I wasn't sure what to expect and thought I might need to attend the class multiple times to get through all I needed to face. The process started with paperwork where I detailed what I'd experienced in life. I knew I'd have to get real with God, be vulnerable in front of these two people, and bring it all to light. I also knew that I didn't want to hold back from God. God was moving in me, and I was willing to let it all go.

I sat with the Lord many nights, working on the things I needed to let out and let go of. I worked on the paperwork and would pray about what I'd written down.

Sometimes it was hard to write it all out, but in my spirit I knew that I had to. I prayed about each thing, and God led me with every word.

I showed up to my first Spiritual Cleansing session with everything filled out and ready to do what needed to be done. I didn't want to hold anything back or waste time holding on to my junk. In the end, that first session was my only session. They didn't have to help me get anything out because God had done the work beforehand. We sat for hours going over all that I'd written. We walked through every area with prayer and tears, then closed the doors to all the junk from my past. I was able to heal that day. As a symbol of closing the door to my past and everything I'd been through in my life, we took the paper and burned it. I was ready to move forward. I wanted to continue my life with purpose.

God doesn't want us to hide what we've been through. If I don't talk about these things about my past, people will never know what God has brought me out of. The things I'm sharing are just a part of my story. I had to learn that God doesn't waste our hurts. Our struggles can be what allows us to help others who've experienced the same hurts, and can become a big part of our purpose. God has a purpose for each of us (Jeremiah 29:11), and it's so much bigger than what we can contain in our minds.

I believe we aren't truly living until we step into our purpose.

# CHAPTER 5

# Into the Wilderness

*A voice of one calling in the wilderness, "prepare the way for the Lord, make straight paths for him."*

**LUKE 3:4 NIV**

Now, did my renewed desire to follow Jesus suddenly make my life completely wonderful and without problems? Nope! For a year and a half after rededicating my life to Jesus as my Savior (I asked God into my heart as a child, and I can look back and see His hand in my life, but this experience was different), I struggled to figure out who I really was and to learn more about Him. I'd been saved, and now I was finally allowing sanctification—letting God mold and change me. Did I get everything right in my life? Nope, but I was working on it.

Sometimes I didn't understand the Bible and I allowed the wrong people to speak into my life because I was still learning and growing and didn't know they were wrong. I thought what they said was true because they said it was in the

Bible or it was religion that had been taught to me. I believed what others told me because I trusted that they knew better since I didn't grow up learning much from the Bible aside from the usual kids' Bible stories. My lack of knowledge caused me to behave legalistically because of my misguided beliefs and attempt to obtain perfection in my own strength. I learned to discern the difference between people's opinion and the truth found in the Bible. I also saw Christians judging those who didn't follow Christ (and those who follow Christ) instead of sharing Gods love to those around them. I was thankful God quickly showed me how that behavior was wrong. He reminded me what He saved me from and that He could do that for anyone. I realized I needed to find out the truth in God's Word for myself.

I also struggled with how some people couldn't see me for the person God was making me into. They still saw who I used to be and all my messy choices. I had thought everyone would be happy that I was changing for the better, but that wasn't always the case. Not everyone wanted to see me doing well, especially if they didn't know God themselves. Since I'd experienced years of different kinds of abuse, it took time for God to walk me through healing in each of those areas. He had healed me from my past, but my thought processes still needed a lot of work. My past had caused some faulty thought patterns in me, and they didn't just go away when I was healed.

Another reality I had to face was knowing that I have a spiritual enemy, just as all who believe in Christ do, and that doesn't exclude those who have not accepted Christ. In John 10:10 Jesus says, "The thief comes only to steal and kill and destroy. I have come so that they may have life and have it in abundance." We are created in God's image, and Satan and his followers' goal is to keep us from seeing the truth and not walking in the ways of the Lord.

Satan doesn't want me to live out my purpose. He doesn't want me to have joy, love, peace, kindness, self-control, healing, goodness, faithfulness, and all the wonderful things God wants for me. He wants to cause confusion, doubt, corruption, and fear. He wants to keep me in bondage, tempt me, make me isolate myself, and keep me in my past. The devil loves to trick us and distract us, and our flesh (our wrong desires, not God desires) can also be deceiving.

But 2 Corinthians 10:3–5 tells us, "For although we live in the flesh, we do not wage war according to the flesh, since the weapons of our warfare are not of the flesh, but are powerful through God for demolition of strongholds. We demolish arguments and every proud thing that is raised up against the knowledge of God, and we take every thought captive to obey Christ." And Ephesians 6:10–11 (NIV) says, "Finally, be strong in the Lord and in his mighty power. Put on the full armor of God, so that you can take your stand against the devil's schemes."

After I got saved, my relationships began to change too. I didn't date for a year and a half, instead wanting to focus on my relationship with God. I did hope to meet someone in the future, though. I was young and wanted a healthy marriage with a man who would love me as much as Christ loves the church.

At the year-and-a-half mark, I met my now husband, Kris, when he was in theology school. I thought we were meant to be because he had a past too; he had been a mess and God took him out of it. Even though he was in theology school when we met, he still continued to struggle with some things. And I came into the relationship with a lot of insecurities and confusion.

We got married a year after we met. When I saw things changing in him (he started picking up old habits before we got married), I thought, *Well, we all have our own walk.* I believed I had chosen to love him, and I let him move into my house before we got married. Because of his past and the changes he'd been making, this way I knew where he was and could help keep him on the right path. That was wrong thinking on my part. My independent self was believing I could fix and control things around me. Even though I'd chosen to follow Christ, I still had a long way to go with my thoughts and how I handled things.

When Kris and I first met, everything seemed so amazing. And when things started going crazy, with him going out and doing things I didn't agree with and us arguing, that actually felt normal even though I didn't want that kind of normal in my life anymore. But when things were healthy, it was nice but also kind of weird because I'd never been in that type of relationship. I would beat myself up inside because I let him live with me before marriage. I would think that God was upset and couldn't use me because I'd messed up. I told myself I should have known better, and believed that I'd lost the purpose He had for me. I felt guilty and insecure and was trying to hold on to God and everything else around me at the same time.

Not long after we got married, Kris and I went through some really hard times. I was hurt deeply by some things that happened, and we both made some wrong decisions. I was angry at Kris. I was angry at God. And I was angry at myself. I would say to God, "I love You, but I don't understand why my life has turned out this way." I thought life would be easier once I chose Christ, and that I'd have more self-control. I thought I'd always put God first. I was so mad at myself for failing Him. Remembering the moments when I fully surrendered my life to Jesus, I couldn't understand why I made decisions that put me in a place where I thought God couldn't use me anymore. It felt like He was far away.

I now realize that I'd taken back the control I'd given to God, and that, in reality, I had no control at all. My thoughts were a mess, my marriage was a mess, and my physical and emotional states were a mess. I would go back and forth with God. I would seek Him, then I'd focus only on my troubles. I'd pray, I'd read His Word, and I'd pursue the joy He'd given me the day I truly chose Him and understood who I was in Christ. But then I'd stop. I was going around and around in a circle in my mind and in my life. It felt like I had a barrier up blocking the full presence of God.

The Lord had freed me from my past—He'd set me on a new path—and here I was doing circles like the Israelites in the wilderness (Deuteronomy 2:3–8) instead of heading to the Promised Land. I was crying out to God, needing Him, thanking Him, and in the next moment I'd be ignoring him and looking at all the wilderness (an empty, pathless area) around me.

The Israelites spent way too much time in the wilderness! They just couldn't keep their focus on God (Exodus 20:3–10). They worshiped other things, they didn't have patience, they always wanted more, and they even said they would have been better off back in slavery in Egypt (Exodus 16:2–3). You know what, though? God was still with them in the wilderness, even despite their complaining and ridiculousness. He provided (Exodus 16:13–18; 17:2, 6), listened when they cried out, and still made promises to them.

I'm thankful that during this time in my life, God surrounded me with friends who loved me. They would listen to me, pray for and with me, and love on me even though I was struggling. They didn't give up on me. They knew my heart desired what God wanted. I was just having trouble seeing clearly because I was allowing my fragmented situation with my husband, and my own guilt and insecurities, to cloud my view of God's sovereignty. They continued to guide me to get my focus back on God.

When I'd keep my eyes on God, I would hear Him and see His guidance. He would give me peace through my storm. But every time I'd take my eyes off Him, the storm would toss me around again. Like Peter walking on the water (Matthew 14:22–33), I'd lock my eyes on Jesus and walk without sinking for a bit, but when my eyes got distracted by the storm and waves, I'd sink down into my emotions again.

God knew which of the women in my life He would use to help me and how. My friend Christine invited me to a two-day women's conference that was about three hours away from Presque Isle, and I knew I needed to go because I felt so defeated and couldn't see past my hurt at the time. I was praying over and over again for healing. Even in the shower getting ready for the event, I kept praying,

"God, please give me healing." The word restore came to my mind, but I continued praying for healing without much thought about it.

> "I'm going to do more than heal you."

During the event, one of the speakers, Paula, used the word restore. I felt my eyes widen and a fire well up inside me. That was the word spoken softly to me in the shower. I knew in my spirit God was speaking. He was saying, "I'm going to do more than heal you."

During the reflection and prayer part of the event, I pondered the word restore and shared what had happened with a wise older woman. She told me that restore didn't mean getting back what I once had, but being given something new. I knew then that the Lord would restore my marriage.

During this same conference, Christine shared a vision she had of me dancing and twirling with the Lord watching over me. She told me I was Daddy's girl. I took that as truth and felt the love of the Lord. It was the first time I knew what it felt like to be a daddy's girl, something I didn't realize I was still longing for. God was showing me how much He loved me and that I was still His girl. Through that conference, God used other women to speak clarity to me when I was having a hard time seeing past my current situation. He was showing me that He was still right there with me.

Sometimes we can't hear God clearly because the problem we're facing is so painful that we allow that pain to take over our thoughts, and we get so focused on praying for the pain to go away that we aren't able to see what God is really doing.

Philippians 1:6 (NIV) tells us, "[We are] confident of this, that he who began a good work in [us] will carry it on to completion until the day of Christ Jesus." He is not done yet! He doesn't just start and stop and give up on us. He put people in my path to do His work, to speak life into me. This is why it matters who you have in your life, spend most of your time with, listen to, and share with. It is important to have people in your life that will point you to Christ, who love as Christ loves, who will pray with and for you. God loves you so much that He will use others to help you.

Ephesians 1:3–4 (NIV) says, "Praise be the God and Father of our Lord Jesus Christ, who has blessed up in the heavily realms with every spiritual blessing in Christ. For he chose us in him before the creation of the world to be holy and blameless in his sight, in love." In Him and His amazing love we are no longer fatherless, alone, and forgotten. We have access to every spiritual blessing! The Lord has chosen you!

## CHAPTER 6

# Major Life Changes

*Have I not commanded you? Be strong and courageous. Do not be afraid; do not be discouraged, for the Lord your God will be with you where you go.*

JOSHUA 1:9 NIV

About a year after Kris and I got married, a coworker of mine who had found her biological dad encouraged me to look for mine. I had already forgiven him even though I didn't know him. Since I had my heavenly Father now and He was all I needed, I didn't feel abandoned by my earthly father anymore. I knew I was a daddy's girl whether I knew my biological dad or not, and what truly mattered to me was that I was loved by God.

Still, I was curious about my biological dad and what he looked like. I was attending the same college that he had graduated from right before I was born, so I decided to see if I could find some information about him there. When I was a teenager, I'd looked for his picture in the yearbooks and hadn't found it, so this time I went to the alumni association. Their spokesperson told me they had no record of a student with the spelling of the name that my mother had given me, but they did have an alumnus with a different spelling of his French last name. I figured it was worth a shot, so I asked for the information.

This happened right around Thanksgiving, and it took me a few days to get up the courage to call the phone number they'd given me. I didn't even know if this man would be the right one or if the phone number was still correct. I didn't know if he had a family or who would answer the phone. I also didn't want to interrupt his life. I wasn't trying to cause harm or get anything from him; I was just curious. I wanted to meet him, even if just once. Kris was so supportive, and with his encouragement, I made the phone call.

I told the man who answered who I was and let him know that I wasn't asking for anything. He asked me a couple questions, then asked if he could call me back. I said yes. That following Friday, after I'd just finished my last client at the hair salon, he called me.

He began talking about not having health issues in the family, and that he was married and had two sons. The whole time, all I could think was, *I'm on the phone with my dad.* I was thirty years old and listening to my dad's voice. We talked for a while and then decided to meet. So many emotions flooded through me that I didn't know what to think.

We planned to meet at a point halfway between our homes, which was about three hours from where I lived. The day of the meeting, our area was supposed to get a big snowstorm, and I worried that the meetup wouldn't happen. The coworker who'd encouraged me to find my dad reassured me that it was going to happen, that he'd travel in a storm to meet me.

Kris and I met him and his wife at an Olive Garden. I had brought a small photo album containing a few pictures of me and Faith, though before we met I wasn't sure whether I would give it to him. I had no idea what we would talk about or how to even start a conversation.

My dad and his wife were very welcoming, though. We talked for a bit, then they handed me a photo album of pictures of him and of my half-brothers. His wife gave me a ring that had been handed down by his grandmother. I couldn't believe it. She (and the rest of the family besides my dad) hadn't known about me, yet she had the heart to give me the ring because I was the first grandchild. I felt so blessed. God had given me my earthly father.

The snowstorm that was supposed to happen followed us as Kris and I traveled home. We never got caught in it. I was so thankful for that day. Not long after, I met my half-brothers, and shortly after that, I met my grandparents, aunts, uncles, and some cousins.

This was difficult for my mother. It brought up a lot of emotions for her, so I tried to keep it separate because I was trying to deal with my own emotions. She knew I wanted to find him and I told her that I talked to him, but I waited to tell her about meeting him till after I met him. I can be very empathetic and I just couldn't handle those feelings with my mom; I needed to just focus on what I was feeling. I know she had doubts about her decisions back when she last saw him, and while I'm sure there's still a lot I don't know about their relationship, that may not be a bad thing; I don't need to know everything.

Not long after I met my father, Kris and I decided to move to South Carolina. My husband was used to moving around, so it didn't bother him, but this was a big deal for me. I had lived in Maine my whole life. I didn't know what it'd be like to leave my family and all that I knew, or what it'd be like to move with my daughter, who was now almost ten years old, and be in a place where I didn't know anyone. All these thoughts made me very anxious. The fear of the unknown was strong, but I also had peace and knew it was what we were supposed to do.

We'd been living in my small trailer in the country, so I had to figure out whether to sell it or rent it. I didn't know if I'd be able to sell it for as much as I owed on it, and I also didn't know how easy it would be to rent it out while living multiple states away. Then I wondered if I'd have to let it go and lose all that I'd worked for. I'd worked hard to purchase my home and provide for my daughter, and I was thankful for all that I had, especially after striving to build my credit back up after my divorce. The thought of leaving it all was difficult to wrap my head around. But God was closing all the doors in Presque Isle. I'd lived there throughout my childhood and young adulthood, but my heart knew it was time for a change.

> ...my heart knew it was time for a change.

I sought the Lord through these emotional struggles. I had women who surrounded me in prayer and supported me as I began to make the transition. I carried verse cards around with me (this was before there were Bible apps for our phones) to help my mind focus on God's Word. I'd pull out those cards, read them, and pray to get myself through the tough times so I wouldn't lose control.

I now see that God needed me to step away from the past so He could show me something new. I needed to be away from old distractions. Stepping out didn't mean I wouldn't be afraid. I was, but I knew moving was what I needed to do.

When Kris and I moved to South Carolina, I thought our marriage would improve, but years of more struggles followed. I knew in my heart that South Carolina was the place we were supposed to be, though, and even in our struggles, God blessed us. He continued working in me even though I battled internally. Kris and I had to start all over again, with a new home, new jobs, a new school for my daughter, and new friendships to build. It all took time. I missed my friends and family, and being able to gather with those I cared about. The difficulty of getting Faith settled was trying. Both she and I wrestled with how big her new school was, and this caused her anxiety and affected her academically. She also had to deal with some bullying.

After living in South Carolina for a year, Faith went into middle school and I started helping out with the youth group at our church. I really enjoyed it and learned a lot, and I thought it'd be great for her to be in a church environment and around church kids. But even at church she felt like she didn't fit in. She'd hang out more with the leaders than with the other kids. Even church kids can be cruel and cliquey, which I understood since I'd experienced the same thing when I was her age, and that caused her to dislike the church.

I really enjoyed working with the youth group, but I felt like I wasn't good enough to be a leader. I still thought Christians had it all together and that none of them were broken and messed up inside like I was. I didn't think anyone else was dealing with what I was dealing with at home—a struggling marriage—and a lot of insecurities rose up in me again. It's funny how things seem because of our misconceptions. God still had a lot to teach me.

I was trying to keep my eyes on Him, though, and I had moments when He spoke so clearly to me. But I also had moments when I felt like my joy was gone. I couldn't take my eyes off my struggles. I was still holding on to anger, bitterness, hurt, unforgiveness, worry, and feelings of worthlessness because of the things I endured in the last couple years of my marriage. God had healed me from so much in my childhood and past traumas, but now I had new things I needed to forgive and let go of. I would look to God, but then go through the same cycle of looking at the things around me and shutting down inside again. There were times when I didn't want to pray because I didn't want to face my pain. It was my old pattern of ignoring it and keeping myself busy and continuing the same circuit in the wilderness.

I felt like things weren't going to change in my marriage, and that I'd messed up so many times with not giving God my all, that God couldn't do much through me anymore. Despite how I thought I'd lost what He had for me, I kept holding on. I was only partially faithful, but God continued to remind me of who He was and who I was in Him.

Kris and I would go back and forth with getting along and not getting along. I went through a couple years not sure if I even loved him anymore. I held on to a lot of anger toward him. We even had a three-month separation. When we got back together, our life together was better, but then it wasn't. We were short with and unkind to each other.

One night while I was at work, my friend's mom came in to get one of her grandchildren's hair cut. We chatted for a while and she asked me how I was doing. I started complaining about my situation. Once before I'd shared some of the things I was struggling with and she'd listened, but this time she looked me in the eye and said, "You need to stop." I immediately knew she was right. I don't recall exactly what she said afterward, but she told me if Kris was trying to do the right thing, then I couldn't keep holding on to the bitterness and have an attitude with him. I needed to let it go and move on. It wasn't fair to him or me. She said that if he chose to do the wrong thing, then I'd know what to do. It was true; I was not being nice to Kris and in return he wouldn't be nice to me. I had a bad and negative attitude that I couldn't see past, but God used her to speak to me. I knew it from the instant she told me to stop.

After she left, I cried and prayed. I knew God had used her to speak to me. I wasn't offended, and I wasn't mad by what she said. Actually, her words pierced my hardened heart. I needed to hear them. When I went home that night, I was different. I treated Kris differently. And because of that, my husband's behavior toward me changed too.

I knew being angry and holding on to bitterness wasn't what I'd wanted. It wasn't who I was. I changed my attitude, and I changed my prayers. I prayed *for* my marriage instead of *against* it. I realized that I had to move forward and not bring up the past, because that kept me stuck in feelings I didn't want to remain in.

> **I changed my attitude, and I changed my prayers.**

I determined to trust God with my marriage and my future.

## CHAPTER 7

# I'm Not Who I Used to Be

*Therefore, there is now no condemnation for those in Christ Jesus, because through Christ Jesus the law of the Spirit who gives life has set you free from the law of sin and death.*

ROMANS 8:1–2 NIV

Even though the Lord gave me freedom from what had kept me captive from my past, I still ended up walking in the wilderness for years. You know that saying that not all who wander are lost? Even though I was in the wilderness, I wasn't lost. As my friend would say, "I was temporarily misplaced." I took some wrong roads and detours and sometimes circled around again, but God was with me the whole time. He knew exactly where I was, and He was preparing me for the day I'd step out of the wilderness. There were times I couldn't see or feel it, but He still protected and provided for me.

Before we moved to South Carolina, I'd gone back to college to finish my associate degree. I still needed ten credits when we moved, so I decided to finish online. After working at a salon for about a year, I decided to open my own business and finish my degree at the same time. (I've always been good at keeping myself busy.) Focusing on my business, I prayed hard about what I should do, what I should name the business, and what my mission would be.

> He grew my awareness and my heart.

God had been moving me in this direction, and Kris played a big part by believing in me and helping me make it happen. I had a lot to learn, but God blessed the business and provided what we needed and the group of people I'd work with. He also brought the right people into my path to show me the community, which allowed me to see beyond just myself to how I could help those around me. That was something I'd never learned growing up. He grew my awareness and my heart.

I continued to seek God and read His Word, Christian living books, and Bible studies. I would cry out during difficult times as a wife and mother—about finances, business, and all the things that life brings. And I would still ask God why I had to face these troubles, and petition God to work in and through me, even though I didn't understand what that might look like. I'd feel great about my relationship with the Lord but then I'd get knocked down with the next thing that came at me. Sometimes I felt like the Israelites wandering in the wilderness for forty years—repenting and worshiping God, but then taking their eyes off Him and worshiping other things. Sometimes I would put my work before God, people before God, things before God. Every time I'd read about them in the Old Testament, I'd think, *Yup, that's me!*

As I continued to study God's Word, I realized that God uses broken people. Despite the wrongs they'd done, these people had faith, and God honored that. He continued to work on my heart and give me a new perspective. I'd thought He was far away from me and that I'd lost the calling He had on my life, but He was right beside me the whole time. I was the one who had built up a brick half wall between us. While I was able to experience a part of Him, maybe feel Him reaching over to help me once in a while, the half wall prevented Him from fully engaging me the way He wanted—and the way I wanted Him to. I wanted the fullness of God.

The main ingredients in bricks are clay, sand, and water (although not all brick types are made of the same substances since local resources vary). The clay becomes strong and holds its shape well once molded and compressed, just like the brick half wall I'd built up during my wandering years. I allowed life experiences to mold and compress me, and placed a strong barrier around the deeper parts of me. I don't think I even realized it at first that I was building a wall.

Sometimes experiences from my past would compel me to build a full wall as if I was protecting myself from more disappointments that might come, and when life would wound me again, I'd begin to build a new wall. But I was not that person anymore who needed to build these walls to protect myself and to hide my insecurities. I needed the presence of the Lord to help tear it down. Eventually, I realized that the wall was keeping me from the most important thing in my life. It held me back from the intimacy with the Lord that I longed for.

The more I would seek the Lord, the more He would show me what I needed to see, hear, feel, and understand. Together He and I would remove one brick at a time. He would show me that I was holding on to bitterness, and I would hand that brick over to Him. He would show me the anger and hurt that I was holding on to, and I would hand another brick over.

He would show me that I wasn't who I used to be. That I wasn't dirty. That I wasn't what others had done to me. And I would hand over those bricks to him.

God showed me that I needed to address my feelings about my family members and others who'd offended or hurt me. I had to see people as He saw them. He showed me that He wasn't done with me, that I was loved. That I wasn't unworthy or not enough. I wasn't stupid. He showed me that I didn't need to fear. That I wasn't a victim. That I wasn't my past or what others—or myself—had labeled me. He showed me that I must forgive.

God would also teach me and guide me in what I needed to let go of—the doubt and disbelief that circled back into my thoughts, my character, and my heart. Each one was a brick I finally was able to hand over to Him. I worked on each brick with the Lord until I gave Him an open path to every part of me. Then He was able to wrap me up in His arms and lift me up with His joy and strength. The clay of my soul was softened so the Lord could mold me into the shape He ordained for my life. He had always been my safe place, my place of joy. Over the years, He has shown me that I can still have joy in all circumstances—and that if I keep my eyes on Him, my joy will remain.

Like the tattoo my aunt had removed, the dark tattoo just below the surface of me was broken up by the light of Christ. Each area of darkness was crushed into pieces and then healed. Scars remained, but they were only on the surface, and they were a reminder of what God did in my life. His light penetrated the deepest, dark things and brought them all to light. It reminded me of Psalm 51:10–12: "God, create a clean heart for me and renew a steadfast spirit within me. Do not banish me from your presence or take your Holy Spirit from me. Restore the joy of your salvation to me, and sustain me by giving me a willing spirit."

In the past, I'd pray to God and say I missed the joy from the day of my salvation back in 2006. That moment would come to my mind, and I'd want that full surrendering awareness and love to fall upon me again. As I continued to let God search me and my heart, He restored me. He reminded me of the day He spoke the word restore over me when I'd been praying for healing. Back then, I'd thought it was just my marriage that He'd restore, but God knew He would need to work on each area of my life over time. He knew I would need not just healing, but restoration. And not just in my marriage, but in my mind, my emotions, and my relationship with Him. This wasn't to restore me to what I once was, or to what I thought my life would look like, but to what I need to be for Him to use me for His purpose and glory.

More of God's Word began to ring true in my life. It was opening up in new ways and I was experiencing His joyous mercies. I am so thankful for God's mercy. His Word is active and alive (Hebrews 4:12) and it was speaking to me. Psalm 34:8 (TPT) says, "Experience for yourself the joyous mercies he gives to all who turn to hide themselves in him." And Psalm 34:8 says, "And see that the Lord is good. How happy is the person who takes refuge in him!"

As God worked in me, my desires changed, as did my prayers. I realized, *If I want more of God, I have to give Him more of me.* Once we accept Christ, He already gives us everything we need, but for me to experience more of Him, I had to give Him more of me. I had to have those vulnerable, get-real moments with God. I didn't want to shut down with God anymore. I didn't want to stop praying, and ignore God every time I was let down or offended in some way. I wanted to keep pressing forward and commit to God's

> **If I want more of God, I have to give Him more of me.**

calling on my life. No more excuses because of doubt, no more holding back from trusting God because I doubted myself and would sometimes feel unworthy of living my life for Him.

God grew my faith, and I experienced deep inner healing. I no longer wanted to wander in the wilderness. I wanted to walk and move in the path and purpose He had given me. The more I read the Word, prayed, and stayed in fellowship with the Lord, the more He strengthened my awareness and showed me the tactics of Satan. Satan couldn't destroy me since I was a believer, but he definitely had a hand in distracting me, manipulating me, and confusing me. Knowing God and His ways, and having an intimate relationship with Him, were my guidance in every area of my life.

Reading God's Word is how we stand firm. It gives us wisdom on how to fight. Just like Peter 5:8–11 (TPT) tells us,

> Be well balanced and always alert, because your enemy, the devil, roams around incessantly, like a roaring lion looking for its prey to devour. Take a decisive stand against him and resist his every attack with strong, vigorous faith. For you know that your believing brothers and sisters around the world are experiencing the same kinds of troubles you endure. And then, after your brief suffering, the God of all loving grace, who has called you to share in his eternal glory in Christ, will personally and powerfully restore you and make you stronger than ever.

Yes, God will set us firmly in place and build us up. He has all the power needed to do this—forever.

# CHAPTER 8

# Out with the Old

*Therefore, if anyone is in Christ, the new creation has come: the old has gone, the new is here!*

**2 CORINTHIANS 5:17**

I used to hold on to everything. Unchecked, I probably could've become a hoarder. I would attach myself emotionally to my belongings and thought that if I let those things go, I might lose the memories of what those things meant to me and reminded me of.

Kris is the total opposite. He sometimes throws out things that he should keep. When we moved to South Carolina, I had to get rid of a lot of stuff, which was extremely hard for me, but I had no choice. We were moving into a small apartment and only had so much space in the moving truck we'd rented. I did begin to make changes during that move. I learned to let things go and get rid of them. At the time, it was emotionally difficult to give many of my belongings away, but afterward I felt a lightness from being free from all that stuff.

Kris taught me how to assess whether I really need each item and to get rid of what isn't necessary. Let's face it, when we leave this earth, someone will need to go through what we've held on to, and I know Faith isn't going to want most of what I have. With Kris's help, I've been able to minimize, although I still have a messy office that my husband dislikes going into. But I have my own organizational system and know where everything is. It's my drop-all space so that the rest of the house won't be. To justify my mess, I remind him about his mess on the counter from time to time. That's one area I really like to keep clean and uncluttered, but he comes in with his stuff and spreads it out on the counter.

Recently, I had a conversation with a client of mine that really stuck with me. This client is an older, retired woman, and she and her husband have lived in their home for many years. She told me that when she buys a new item for the house, she gets rid of an old item. If she's not willing to get rid of an old item, then she doesn't get the new one. She knows her children won't want all her stuff, and she doesn't want to add more things that are not needed.

The other day I went clothes shopping, and on the way home I thought about what my client had shared. In my bedroom with my bags of new clothes, I looked in my closet and started taking out the clothes I either hadn't worn in a long time or that I'd worn many times but wasn't going to wear again. It was time to retire them. I even found a couple of new-with-tags shirts I'd forgotten about since they were hidden between all the other clothes.

This motivated me to move on to my dresser drawers, which were stuffed full. I always end up wearing the same clothes, so the other clothing just sits in the drawer and gets a funny smell. I never understood why clean clothes get smelly from just sitting in a drawer, so I looked it up online and found a site called ClosetAmerica that says the odor is usually due to storing clothes in tight spaces that aren't well ventilated, are dark and dusty, or include smelly shoes or dirty clothes. Their recommendation for avoiding smelly clothes is to have an organized, well-designed closet. [1]

So I went through every drawer and ended up filling a couple of garbage bags with clothes. Then I reorganized my closet and put all my new clothes lined up together in the middle front so I would see them easily and actually wear them. All the drawers got reorganized too, which resulted in more room and made finding what I want much easier. The whole process was so satisfying.

Now, why am I talking about clothing organization? Because our minds work the same way. We keep holding on to the old junk cluttering our thoughts with things we should've gotten rid of. These thoughts are old and worn out, don't fit us, and take up room even though they're not needed anymore. And because of them, we can't make appropriate room for the good new things we need to put in our head. These good new things get lost in the junk that's just sitting there getting stinky.

Then, when we open that overstuffed drawer and the stinky clothes pop out and we can't get it closed again—that's just like what we do in our life. We hold on to too many things. We stuff them back in and think we'll deal with them another day, but when we're overwhelmed, we eventually show our stink when we can't stuff anything else in. We have

**We need to get a fresh look, a fresh perspective.**

to declutter, get organized, and develop a well-designed thought pattern. We need to get a fresh look, a fresh perspective.

God has had to remap my thoughts from the old ways of thinking, seeing, and hearing to the new ways of Him. When troubles or disappointments come, I don't want to sit in my head in misery anymore. I did that for way too long. Now, I stop my thought pattern and take it to God.

Years ago, a pastor's wife shared with a group of us an answer her husband had given her when she asked him, "How can I control the thoughts that come?" He said, "You can't always control the thoughts that come, but you can choose to replace them." That has always stayed with me. I choose to replace my thoughts with truth—and how do I know what truth is? By reading God's Word and being in communication with the Lord daily.

We can also think of these thoughts as weeds. I had a lot of overgrown weeds in my head, and I needed to remove them for God's seeds of truth to grow without being stuffed out or restrained. As I began my journey of changing my thought patterns and pulling weeds, I had to ask myself some questions.

Who is God to me, and does my belief about that line up with who God really is?

Who do I say I am, and who does God say I am?

I want you to ask yourself these same questions.

We just did a study at church with one of our pastors, Tim Roberson, who put together this study called "Hearing the Voice of God." In one of the sessions, he talked about the attributes of God and gave us a list of names and attributes of God that he had found at www.biblenamesofgod.com. Knowing who God truly is helps us to see things the way He sees them, and that includes how we see ourselves.

What I learned is that God has unlimited power. He is everywhere at the same time and knows everything. He is unchanging. He is infinite, eternal, and limitless. He is divine, without sin, perfect, and pure. He is Spirit. He is righteousness and goodness. He is love. He is holy, faithful, the author of life, the Alpha and Omega. He is our advocate. He is our deliverer, heavenly Father, helper, counselor, redeemer, forgiver, truth sayer, rock, and glorious friend. He is light, compassion, and graciousness. He is our healer and our Savior. I could add many more attributes of God, but to me, He is my everything.

Genesis 1:27 tells us, "God created man in his own image; he created him in the image of God; he created them male and female." Since God made us in His own image, what does that say about us? And if God is all these things, and He created us in his own image, shouldn't we think that way about ourselves?

I used to believe that I was less than, that I wasn't enough. I felt shameful, dirty, stupid, fat, ugly, hidden, outcast, and unloved. I thought I was broken and unfixable. I thought I had to do things on my own and that I didn't need anyone else. I thought I'd be my own strength and that I'd just settle with being in the dark of my self-pity, that I wouldn't be anything but labeled broken. But when I set my mind on who God is and what He says about us in His Word, I can see that those thoughts weren't His thoughts.

Romans 8:1–2 says, "Therefore, there is now no condemnation for those in Christ Jesus, because the law of the spirit of life is in Christ Jesus has set you free from the law of sin and death." Verse 5 in this chapter says, "For those who live according to the flesh have their minds set on the things of the flesh, but those who live according to the spirit have their minds set on the things of the spirit." And verse 11 says, "And if the spirit of him who raised Jesus from the dead lives in you, then he who raised Christ from the dead will also bring your mortal bodies to life through his spirit who lives in you."

When we choose Christ, He lives in us! We no longer have to hold on to those thoughts and feelings! The definition of *condemned* is "sentenced to a particular punishment, especially death; officially declared unfit for use."[2]

I felt unfit for use for most everything throughout most of my childhood and a lot of my adulthood. I thought I would just work and live life, but not anything beyond that. I never thought God could use me for His glory. But God's Word tells me I'm His. Jeremiah 29:11 tells us that God has a plan and purpose for our lives. It's not to harm us, but to give us hope and a future. I'm not unfit for use, and neither are you! I'm not sentenced for disaster, and neither are you! He says that when we call on Him, He will listen (1 John 5:14–15). He says that when we seek Him with all our heart, we will find Him (Jeremiah 29:13). This assures me that I'm not alone. That I don't have to do it alone. That He will guide me. He already knows the path He has planned for me. This is true for you as well!

1 Corinthians 5:17 tells us, "Therefore, if anyone is in Christ, he is a new creation. The old has passed away; behold the new has come." How exciting! I'm not who I once was. The old has passed and the new has come.

God chose us, and through Christ Jesus we've been redeemed. I'm a child of God (I'm not fatherless), I'm a friend of God (I can have an intimate relationship with Him daily, and I can depend on Him), I'm forgiven (I can have freedom), I'm a masterpiece (I'm not ugly, stupid, damaged, or broken), I'm loved (I'm not unloved or forgotten), and I'm His ambassador (His light resides in me and shines in and through me, so I no longer live in darkness).

The more I pray, read God's Word, listen, and obey His promptings in my life, the more I can grasp who God is and who I am. I can clean out the stinky, old clothing from my closet and dresser and replace them with the fresh, new, fragrant pureness of Christ.

It takes a choice to change our perspective and make those changes in our life. It's our choice to tear down the walls and hand over the bricks. It's our choice to reorganize so we fit God's design for our life.

> **It's our choice to reorganize so we fit God's design for our life.**

As another example, I'm being stubborn about my age and what my body wants to do even though I don't want to accept it. I started using reading glasses when I turned forty, which I wasn't happy about, but I needed them. A couple of years later, seeing my client's hair clearly became difficult, especially in the evening. So I had to get glasses for distance as well. I ended up wearing glasses all the time.

When I went to the eye doctor last year, they increased my prescription and added a little for distance, even though I didn't really see much difference. But this year, I can tell the difference when I don't wear my glasses for distance, and I can see a shift in my up-close vision when I do wear my glasses. Still, I canceled my yearly check-up. I didn't want to know if I need a stronger prescription. I'm keeping what I have for now. In a nutshell, I'm choosing not to see as clearly as I could. The reason for this is my pride. Part of me asks, *How can I have pride when in the past I thought such horrible things about myself?* But the pride I carry says that I can do things on my own and I will do my best to be the best I can be. Maybe it's a little vanity, thinking that I'm not old enough for all this. Trust me, God lets me know that I need Him when I behave this way.

We do the same thing with Christ sometimes. He has everything that we need to see clearly, but many times we choose not to pursue it. We can be stubborn and unwilling to accept something or give something up. We just don't want to go see "the doctor." We'd rather sit in the tornado of our circumstances. This is when we need a shift in our perspective and to meet with the One who can give us clear vision.

## CHAPTER 9

# Forgiveness

*Set your minds on things above,
not on earthly things.*

**COLOSSIANS 3:2**

Forgiveness—giving it and receiving it—is crucial. In my life particularly, I had to face my inability to forgive. God had given me healing from my past and He showed me that I still had to forgive those who hurt me, but I also needed to forgive myself. Not just say it, but truly search my heart and ask God to help me forgive.

Forgiving myself for my failures as a mom, and for the mistakes I made along the way in relationships and in friendships, may have been harder than forgiving others. While I don't have to daily face others who've I've forgiven, I do have to face myself. I still have times when I think about the ways I've messed up and wish I'd made better choices, especially as a mom. I did things that hurt people I care about, which can be difficult to deal with even years later. I've asked God to cover those areas I failed at as a mom and to work in the lives of the people who've been affected by my actions. I've prayed that God would fill the areas in my daughter that I missed the opportunity to fill. I've prayed that if I'd failed as a mom, wife, daughter, or friend, that God would bring healing to those affected. I can't go back and change the past, but I know who can heal it and who has my—and my loved ones'—present and future in His hands. I know a powerful God who can reach those who seem unreachable. I know a God who can break through the hardness I may have caused in my child. And I know I can trust God to do what I couldn't.

I also know that while God has forgiven my sins, people may not always forgive me. Maybe you've experienced that as well. It's something we're not able to control. We can do everything in our power to ask for forgiveness and try to make up for our failures, but, ultimately, we have to put the situation into the hands of the One who's powerful enough to handle what we can't.

We have to do the same thing with those who we've struggled to forgive. Forgiveness is not always a one-time thing. With each offense against us, we must offer forgiveness so we don't hold on to the offense and allow it to be something that can hinder us. Unforgiveness can cause bitterness, anger, depression, anxiety, and even physical issues with our body. We can actually let something stew in us until it causes harm and that turns into emotional, spiritual and sometimes physical bondage. We can make ourselves physically sick by holding onto things that we shouldn't. How many times do studies and doctors tell us that stress causes physical ailments. I see it in my career; when people are over stressed, they can lose their hair. What we hold onto and don't address can affect so many areas of our soul, body, and mind. We must forgive as Christ forgave us (see Ephesians 4:31–32).

I recently had a conversation with Faith about forgiveness. She asked me about a friend who I'd had a falling out with. While she didn't know all the details, she saw that I still had some contact with her. I explained that we were in groups together and everything was fine between us, but we don't have the relationship we once had—that it's better that way. "You know me, I forgive people easily," I told her.

She responded that that must be why she forgives people easily too, and why she lets them back into her life and then gets hurt and taken advantage of. I shared that I used to do the same thing but that forgiving doesn't mean forgetting about what's happened and allowing wrongful behavior to continue. We can forgive a person but also refuse to allow their toxic behavior back into our life. Boundaries are important in every relationship, and some people's actions may be so problematic that we need to remove them from our life. Either way, forgiveness takes away the power of affliction.

> ...forgiveness takes away the power of affliction.

Forgiving someone doesn't mean we magically forget what happened. I have a lot of memories of past abuse, past hurts, and past failures, but I choose not to ruminate on those memories. They happened, but I don't dwell on the details anymore. If my mind starts sitting in the past, I take those thoughts and lay them at the feet of Jesus and remember all He has done in my life. Why would I want to go back to the past when I know what it's like to walk in freedom from it? I don't live in bondage anymore.

I'm claustrophobic, and just thinking about someone locking me in a closet or in a small space I can't get out of makes me freak out inside. My thoughts freeze up, and I feel out of control and like I can't breathe. My first reaction is to want to punch and kick my way out. And if someone unlocked and opened the door, I would run out and never go near that small space again.

Yet so many times in our lives we go back to the same place—whether physical or emotional—that took our breath and made us freeze up and lose control. This is when we can choose to forgive, remember what God gave us freedom from, and hand over the key to God. Once we know what freedom in Christ feels like, we want to continue to walk in that freedom.

The Bible has a lot to say about forgiving others. Colossians 3:13 says, "[Bear] with each other and [forgive] one another if anyone has a grievance against another. Just as the Lord has forgiven you, so you are also to forgive." And Luke 6:37 says, "Do not judge, and you will not be judged. Do not condemn, and you will not be condemned. Forgive, and you will be forgiven." When I think about what God has forgiven me for, I'm able to ask Him to help me see others as He sees them, and to help me forgive.

In the middle of the pain Christ endured on the way to be crucified and on the cross, He said, "Father, forgive them, because they do not know what they are doing" (Luke 23:34). Christ laid down his life for us and, in the middle of being tortured, He still forgave and asked God to forgive those who were doing Him harm. He endured and forgave so that we could be saved. That tells me that no matter what, I must forgive others. I had to forgive Mr. M. I had to forgive my mom, my dad, my past boyfriends, my ex-husband, and anyone else who'd wronged me.

I once had a conversation with Faith about praying for her father. When I mentioned to her I forgave him, she responded with something like, "Yeah, right." That's when I shared with her why I pray for him. I pray for him because I know God loves and wants him just as much as He loves and wants me or anyone else. And if her father changed due to the power of Christ and walked in the ways of the Lord, what an example that would be for Faith, and he could reach people in the way God had designed him to.

Forgiveness allows the difficult things we face—in the past and the present—to not have power over us. The only power I want in my life is the amazing power of Christ. I also want that for others! It is what brings healing and transformation in someone. In my life today, I really don't think about my past. So when writing this book, when I had to think about all the things I have gone through and all the feelings I use to feel, it was really hard to put myself back there and to be clear in my writing of all the things I've faced in my life. I knew it was for a purpose, though, and now I'm focused on my present and what God is leading me to.

Just the other day, I was in my prayer time and God brought Faith's father to my mind. I began to pray for him and felt God's presence and my spirit knew God was going to move in his life. I felt such joy. Now that is all God! This man is someone who hurt me deeply in my past, but I can see that God is going to move in his life and that brought me joy. That is the power of Christ! That's what only God can do. Praying for our enemies and those who hurt us is such a powerful thing (see Matthew 5:43–45).

## CHAPTER 10

# Revisiting the Past But Not Living In It

*Forget the former things; do not dwell on the past. See I am doing a new thing! Now it springs up; do you not perceive it? I am making a way in the wilderness and streams in the wasteland.*

**ISAIAH 43:18-19**

When God put it on my heart to share my story, I didn't get serious about it as quickly as I could have. I would start and stop for all kinds of reasons, whether it was making time to write, dealing with the emotions I knew I'd have to face, or wondering how to write the book or whether I was even capable of doing it. I would think of my weaknesses, like not spelling words correctly and not expressing my feelings well at times.

One thing I was sure of, though, is that if God calls us to something, He will provide all that we need to complete it. So I chose to get serious. I knew writing this book would be a new journey as I poured my life, my heart, and my faith onto paper, but I was ready even though I had fears to face. Being vulnerable opens the door for judgment from others. I know people may reject me or want to debate my words. And people may bring up things from my past.

As well, my insecurities may rise up at times. I'm human and still a work in progress. I don't always get things right. Despite how far I've come, I know I'll always be learning and allowing God to work on me—until the day I leave this earth.

But what outshines my fears is knowing that hearts will be reached with the hope that Jesus brings. If my opening up and sharing causes some to judge me, so be it. If my life experiences and what I've learned from them are able to help others, it'll be worth it.

By opening up, I also receive freedom and a new sense of purpose. I can point others to the One who saved me even when I seemed unsavable. Psalm 34:5 tells us, "Those who look to him are radiant with joy; their faces will never be ashamed." And 2 Corinthians 10:5 (NIV) says, "We demolish arguments and pretension that sets itself up against the knowledge of God, and take captive every thought to make it obedient to Christ."

While I was writing this book, I took a trip back to Maine to see family and friends. Faith and I usually do this once a year. I love this time with her because she's an adult now and I don't get to see her much since she has a full-time job and lives with her friends. I love having her as my travel buddy, and it doesn't hurt that she's a lot better with directions than me.

Although visiting family is exciting for me, I also get anxious knowing that some painful feelings and emotions always surface when I'm there. This time, I kept playing over in my head what I wanted to do when I got there—how I'd plan to make time to see everyone and how I'd make enough quality time with family and friends but also do some of the things I enjoyed, like hiking and kayaking.

I also worried about my emotions and didn't want to get stuck in or distracted by them. There's usually some kind of family drama while I'm there, and I wanted to avoid that as much as possible. Each year, it seemed like I'd always get sucked in and then have to try to protect myself. That made it difficult to enjoy my time because I was too busy trying to avoid things, keep my boundaries up, and make everyone happy.

One of my friends has always encouraged me to let Christ's light shine through me while I'm there, but each year I would feel like I failed at it. I thought, *How can I let my light shine when I keep the wall up around me to protect myself from unwanted emotions?* Still, this year I prayed continually for my trip. I asked God to help me to just enjoy my family. I wanted Him to help me see them the way He does, and to use me while I was there. I prayed for life-giving conversations. These petitions continued during my visit.

I always held the belief that God couldn't use me in the area where I'd grown up. I'd think about how the people of Nazareth rejected Jesus and His teaching. In Luke 4, the people even threatened his life. "But he passed right through the crowd and went on his way" (v. 30). While what I experienced wasn't even close to that, I found myself thinking, *This isn't my home anymore. This isn't my mission field. This isn't the place for me to make a difference.*

During this trip everything was going well. Our flight went smoothly and arrived early, and we started out at my biological dad and his fiancée's house (several years prior, he'd gotten divorced from the wife I'd met). The next morning while having coffee and chatting with them, I told them about writing this book and some of the things God had been doing in my life. I hadn't planned to share this yet, but God opened the door and I was thankful to share my heart. While they didn't say much, they showed interest and my dad's fiancée asked several questions.

Afterward, Faith and I headed to the Bar Harbor area to see more family, especially my aunt and uncle who I lived with the summer after high school. They have always been so good to me, and we always have a great time when we get together. While we were there, I wanted to go hiking in Bar Harbor, so the next day my uncle and I went. He took me on a trail with beautiful views, then we drove around and checked out some other areas he knew on Mt. Desert Island. The day turned out much better than I'd even expected.

The next day Faith and I headed north to Presque Isle, where my mom, my sister, and many other family members live. This year marked fourteen years since we had moved away. One day faith was with her dad, so I met with my mom, sister, niece, and great-niece for lunch. I hadn't seen Jen in two years, and since we aren't able to keep in touch otherwise, I only get to catch up with her when I visit. We were close during our teenage and early adult years but then grew apart due to personal issues.

Jen and I usually talk about the past when we get together, and this visit, she and I talked for a few hours. Some of the things she said and her better outlook on dealing with our childhood made it clear that she'd been in therapy, which I was thankful for. Although she was usually the one to do the talking (and never held back or sugarcoated anything) while I didn't say much, this time we both talked openly.

We talked and shared, getting teary-eyed at times, and Mom just listened. Jen then shared some things I didn't remember. She also told me about how she found out about Mr. M sexually abusing me and about some of the things she had to work through in therapy. We side-eyed Mom, and she said she'd need therapy after just sitting there. (Mom has been through a lot in her life and it's affected her in multiple ways.) Though we talked about the past, it ended up being a good visit and I was happy we got to catch up.

That weekend, I went to my aunt and uncle's camp at Long Lake, about an hour north of Presque Isle, with them. We went on the ATV trails, ate good food, played cards (I won!), laughed, and had a great time. On the last day at the camp, my cousin and I went kayaking on the lake and talked and talked. It was a Sunday, and we had church right there on the water.

For years I'd been praying for God to touch the lives of my family. That day I saw just that. It was a cloudy morning, but as we sat on the water pouring our hearts out and talking about God, the clouds opened and gave us a moment of sun and a fresh presence of God. My heart was so full as I looked at this young woman who'd always meant so much to me. I encouraged her with what God had laid on my heart for her, and to this day it excites me to think about what He is going to do through her. When I left camp and headed for my friend's house, where I'd be staying next, I was in such awe of what God was showing me and what He was doing in the lives of those around me.

My childhood friend whose home I would be staying at was going to be gone for a couple of days, and Faith was shuffling back and forth between her dad's place and my mom's house, so that was the first night and morning that I was alone since the trip started. I really needed that time. In the morning I got up and started reading *The Awe of God: The Astounding Way a Healthy Fear of God Transforms Your Life* by John Bevere. It was the new study our sisterhood at church was getting ready to start, and it was the perfect book to read in the middle of experiencing some awe-inspiring God moments. I also looked over my notes that I was going to share at my outdoor Walk by Faith group about not looking back, which seemed so fitting since I was back in the area where I'd grown up. I was revisiting my past but not reliving it.

> **I was revisiting my past but not reliving it.**

That day I planned to climb Haystack Mountain. I hoped that I'd have cell reception up there so I'd be able to do a live video on our group page and share my teaching/study from the top of the mountain. But as I was getting ready to leave, my friend's mother-in-law, whom I adore, walked in the door. I knew she'd be coming by sometime that day, and she was so excited to see me. I let her know that I was about to leave to go climb Haystack, and she went and sat on the porch while I finished packing my backpack.

When I went outside, she asked if I could pray for her since she had some difficult things going on in her life and had recently had a health scare. So I sat with her and began to pray, but then I felt the need to stop. I did and asked her if she'd experienced a prayer like this before. She said she hadn't, so I asked her if she'd ever asked Jesus into her heart, and she said no. I asked her if she wanted to, and she immediately said yes. So I walked her through doing that.

This was another awe-inspiring God moment! We sat and talked for a while, and she told me she'd been praying that I would be at the house when she arrived. God heard her prayer. It was His perfect timing—His unexpected pause when we stop our planned direction and walk the direction He is guiding us to.

When I finally left for the mountain, I was praising God as I pondered what just happened. It was in that moment I realized that God was showing me that no matter where I'm at, He can still use me. He had shifted my perspective again. I'd been praying to have a life-giving conversation with someone back home, and what's more life-giving than praying with someone and hearing them confess and ask Jesus to come into their heart? I felt so very blessed to experience this incredible moment with her.

There were other sweet times during that trip too, and I came home without holding on to any of the stressful moments. Those amazing God moments outweighed the things that just didn't matter. In the past, I'd often still feel out of sorts for a while after I returned to South Carolina, but not this year. God showed me a new way to see things.

The more I share my anxieties and thoughts with God and release them and not hold back, the more my heart desires what He desires, and the more I step into the plans and purpose He has for me. We all have a purpose. Our common purpose is to build the kingdom of God and to bring Him glory, and then we have individual purposes that are determined by the gifts He's given us.

No matter your past, no matter what you have done, the Lord has created you with a purpose, and He will guide you into what He has for you. If you seek Him, pray, and ask for His guidance, He will show you the gifts He has given you and how to use them to do His work.

You are unique, and God chose you (Psalm 139:16; Ephesians 2:10). You have a place of influence because of who you are and how God created you.

> You have a place of influence because of who you are and how God created you.

He prepared in advance His purpose for you. Listen for His voice so that you know the path to take. He will give daily guidance in your place of work, your home, your children, your finances, your community, and your church—He will guide in all things. (Psalm 32:8; Isaiah 58:11).

Isaiah 32:3 (NIV) says, "Then the eyes of those who see will no longer be closed, and ears of those who hear will listen." Ask for wisdom, and open your heart, your eyes, and your ears and listen to God. See yourself as He sees you. Romans 12:6 (NIV) tells us, "We all have different gifts, according to the grace given to each of us." If your gift is prophesying, then prophesy in accordance with your faith; if it is serving, then serve; if it is teaching, then teach; if it is to encourage, then give encouragement; if it is giving, then give generously; if it is to lead, do that diligently; and if it is to show mercy, do it cheerfully. First Peter 4:10 (NIV) says, "Each of you should use whatever gift you have received to serve others, as faithful stewards of God's grace in its various forms."

It is never too late to grasp hold of what God created you for. I had thoughts in my past that it was too late for me. But that was a lie I believed for too long. If you think that about yourself, it's also a lie. Stop believing that lie today and determine to believe and receive the truth about what God says about you. You have purpose, you have gifts, and you are chosen. There's no greater joy than to do the work God has created us to do.

## CHAPTER 11

# Rooted

*Rooted and built up in him, strengthened in the faith as you were taught, and overflowing with thankfulness.*

**COLOSSIANS 2:7 NIV**

In chapter 5 I talked about how it matters who you have in your life, spend most of your time with, listen to, and share with. It is important to have people in your life that will point you to Christ, who love as Christ loves, who will pray with and for you. God loves you so much that He will use others to help you.

I want to talk about this a little more because it has been a struggle for me, my place of pride. It's the "I don't need anyone" attitude—or "I don't want to bother anyone," "I don't want to put my feelings on anyone," or "I can just do it myself." I lived my life for years figuring things out myself, not having help, and making things work the best I could. God is still working with me on this. Sometimes I have stubborn moments when I won't let my husband help me because "I can do it myself." Let me give you an example of how ridiculous I can be—and trust me, my husband will tell me that's how I am being.

Kris and I live on three acres of land and we have a lot of vegetation. The lady that owned the house before us was a professional gardener, so she had so many plants and bushes, and it was beautiful. But we found out very quickly how much work it was to keep up with the yard work. Kris likes a very simple and clean looking yard, so we removed tons of trees, bushes, and plants.

One day I had this one dead-looking bush that needed to come out, and I got my gloves on and grabbed down at the bottom of the bush and started pulling. This bush would not budge. So I got out a sharpshooter shovel and started chopping away at the roots. I needed to break up as many roots as I could so I could then pull the bush out of the ground.

I was sweating and getting frustrated at this stupid bush while my husband was also working somewhere in the yard. But I refused to go ask him for help. I continued to break up as many roots as I could and reached back down to the bottom of the bush and pulled with all that I had left. The bush still had a strong root and would not let loose from the ground. As I was pulling with all my body weight, some branches broke and I flew back and landed on my butt, with the bush still standing firm in the ground. I finally gave in, and went and found Kris to come and help me. We both got a good grip at the bottom area of the bush and pulled that deep-rooted bush out with one pull! Had I asked him sooner, I wouldn't have landed on my butt.

Sometimes the bushes in our life have some deep roots to them. The bush started out as a seed that we wished had never been planted to begin with, but we let it grow to the point it had a firm root system. On my own I couldn't remove it. I could try some within my own strength to break up the roots and tackle what I could, but ultimately I had to ask for help. I needed help because this bush was well established, but it was not something that I wanted to maintain any longer.

Likewise, we need Jesus and we need those people in our life who will reach down in the dirt with us. People who will pray, and point us to Jesus. We can't save each other, but we can point each other to the one who can—Jesus Christ.

We need to be rooted in Christ. I know some people have a hard time with church, religion, or God, and that may be because of past experiences with church, or man-made religion, or whatever has tainted their view. I've had a lot of these feelings myself with churches and religion. I have felt judged and not welcome, and was not always taught the correct things when it comes to the truths in God's Word. But I have also experienced the goodness of having people who love Christ, love on me, and help me in times of need.

The church I go to has provided a place for me to grow in my faith. I've been with this church since we moved to South Carolina in 2009, and since then I've watched as the church has expanded to multiple locations in the Lowcountry. I started attending their main campus and then years later decided to transfer to their north campus. In 2018 Kris and I moved to the country, and after a year of traveling fifty minutes to the north location, I finally listened to God and transferred to their Ridgeville location. I love my church, and when I say that, I'm not talking about the building; I'm talking about the people (see 1 Corinthians 12:27–28).

Over the years, I've learned how important a community of believers is and that we aren't meant to do life alone. Hebrews 10:25 tells us that God calls believers to meet together for encouragement. I had a dream the other night, and even though I can't remember the entire dream, I remember waking up knowing that God was showing me that I shouldn't fight my battles alone. That was so clear in my mind. I had been struggling with some things, and though I did take them to God, I was still battling alone. I thought no one needed to know what I was dealing with. You know, that same pride pattern of "I don't want to bother anyone" or "I don't want to keep asking for the same prayer request."

But God has given me some core people in my life who've helped me to know better than to have those thoughts. If I ask them to pray, they will and won't mind. If I need them, they will be right there for me. And if they ask me for prayer or need me to show up for them, I will. I do like to be on the end of helping and praying for others than asking for help and prayers.

We all need core people who we can share our lives with, people who lift us up in prayer and encourage us. Romans 12:15 tells us to rejoice with those who rejoice and mourn with those who mourn. We should always take our cares and concerns to God first, but when battles are hard, there's power in prayer and there's power in numbers. This is why we need each other. Satan loves to isolate us, confuse us, and make us think we don't need anyone else, but we aren't meant to do life alone.

When it comes to fighting battles, praising God is the best weapon we have. This is true especially when we don't know what to pray for or don't have the words. We praise Him for what He has done for us and others in our life. We praise Him for His faithfulness, His promises, His grace, His power, and His creation. Even if we don't feel like it. Praising Him has a way of shifting our perspective. This is when we can reach out to the that friend who will lift us up in prayer and encouragement. They can praise with us.

Also important when fighting spiritual battles is using the Word of God. Anything we read or hear should be vetted using the Bible. This means we need to read the Word and know it. Before reading the Bible, we should ask God to reveal it to us. Knowing God's Word and being in a relationship with God will keep us from being deceived. And the relationship is crucial. Many people know the Bible but lack the relationship part. Knowing about someone—God, in this case—is not the same as actually knowing someone. And if we've strayed, we can always reconnect with God. He never moved away in the first place (see Psalm 34:18).

Through the church I've met some close friends, and been able to be fed by God's Word, to get confirmation when God spoke something in areas of my life, to be convicted, and to learn, grow, and be encouraged. I've also been able to be the encourager and used for God's purposes. First John 4:7 says we show God's love by loving others.

A sad situation that sometimes happens in a church is what we often call "church hurt." While the church is God's house, it's run by people—flawed people. We all deal with difficult things in our lives, and that affects how we interact with others. As well, we have different personalities and sometimes different views on things. For these reasons, people can be hurt by those they attend church with or sit under the leadership of. I've had it happen, and I know many others have as well.

When this happens, we need to remain faithful to what God is asking us to do. In my case, God had me face the person multiple times. He even had me sit under leadership of this person for a short period. He had me stay silent when this person talked about me. It was hard. Really hard. But I was constantly reminded that what God was doing was bigger and more important than me. I didn't want to let my emotions get in the way of God reaching the people who needed to be reached—or in the way of Him teaching me what He wanted me to learn. If God could use me to help someone else, I wanted to be a part of that.

During this time, I had a lot of conversations with God so I could stay focused on Him. I chose to write all the things that were said, and the hurt that was caused, in my journal. I prayed over it and told God I wanted to leave it there on the paper so I'd no longer run the details of it through my mind. I also needed to check myself and make sure my heart was right.

Despite this situation, I'm so incredibly thankful for the church. We need a faith community around us. Even in the hurt, even in the circle of imperfect people. None of us are perfect, and in the same way I hope people will give me grace for my not-so-perfect ways, I hope I can give grace in the same way. That said, if you're a part of a church that you find is not following God's Word, leaving may be necessary. Seek God's wisdom and be obedient to what He says. Sometimes, for our own good, we need to move on from people, and sometimes we need to move on from a church. Just don't move on from God! Move toward Him.

## CHAPTER 12

# Repentance Brings Restoration

*He removed the foreign altars and the high places, smashed the sacred stones and cut down the Asherah poles.*

**2 CHRONICLES 14:3 NIV**

This year I've started studying God's Word in a new way, digging deep and praying about each thing God has shown me in the promises He has for me and for my family. Over the years, He's taught me to take my thoughts off myself and turn my attention to those around me. In my own struggles of being a wife, a mom, and a business owner, and dealing with disappointments and distractions as a result, I still pray for others and want them to experience the presence of God. When I pray for others, I see God move in my life and in others' lives.

Through my studying of God's Word and prayer, I've been able to share monthly with an outdoor women's group I started in January 2023. This group was something God put on my heart, and I wasn't sure what He was going to do with it, but I decided that each month I'd share a topic and supporting verses. I would read the Bible and ask God, "What do you want me to talk about this month?" and He would give me a topic. I'd ask Him what verses, and as I would read His Word, He would show me the verses and what I needed to learn and share.

I didn't try to plan the whole year but instead took it month by month, allowing God to work. I would be in prayer and make sure it was Him leading, because I never wanted it to be me. I'm human and I mess up, but I trust God and have faith that He will do what I cannot do. Some of the topics have been "a place of survival," "He hears our cries," "His promises," "His works in our weaknesses," "wisdom," and "understanding." I'm now on "repentance brings restoration." I want to share "repentance brings restoration" with you because it really connects with what brings us to that place of fullness with God—a place I've found myself in over and over again.

A passage in 2 Chronicles 12 really stuck out to me. After Solomon dies and his son Rehoboam becomes king, the kingdom is divided. Rehoboam doesn't seek the Lord about anything, and he listens to the wrong people and abandons the law of the Lord. He's nothing like David or Solomon. Then, when Rehoboam and his leaders learn that they will be destroyed, they humble themselves:

> So the leaders of Israel and the king humbled themselves and said, "The LORD is righteous." When the LORD saw that they had humbled themselves, the LORD'S message came to Shemaiah: "They have humbled themselves; I will not destroy them but will grant them a little deliverance. My wrath will not be poured out on

Jerusalem through Shishak. However, they will become his servants so that they may recognize the difference between serving me and serving the kingdoms of other lands." (vv. 6–8)

The words *little deliverance* stuck out to me. The King James Version says "some deliverance." "Humbled themselves" means they lowered themselves in dignity or importance—they renounced any pride or arrogance.

The leaders of Israel accepted that God was righteous and that He would judge accordingly, so they humbled themselves because they didn't want to be destroyed. God delivered them a little bit. Verse 8 says that He didn't destroy them completely. He let them know what it was like to serve other kingdoms over serving God. And verse 14 says Rehoboam did what was evil because he didn't determine in his heart to seek the Lord.

This led me to question myself, and maybe this is a question for you too: Do I want to be delivered just a little, just some?

> **Do I want to be delivered just a litte, just some?**

No, I want to be rescued, to be saved. I want to be rescued from bondage, set free, and delivered from evil and corruption and all that holds me back from the joy of the Lord. Humbling myself has put me in a place where God could work in me, and it made me teachable. Being humble is so important; it can allow growth to happen. But what Rehoboam and his people really needed was to repent and seek the Lord. Repentance brings restoration!

Repentance is the action of repenting—of showing sincere regret and remorse. It's a change of direction. Restoration is the act of repairing, rehabilitating, rebuilding, reconstructing, and redecorating something to a good condition or operation. It's to return or turn back. Rebirth. The action of returning something to a former owner, place, position, or condition.

During the reign of Rehoboam, and later his son Abijah, things didn't change because they had abandoned the Lord. But when Abijah's son Asa became king, the direction shifted (2 Chronicles 14). Asa did what was right in the sight of the Lord. He removed the Israelites' idols and anything else that needed to be taken out of the kingdom so they could follow God's ways. He told the people to seek the Lord and follow His commands. The Israelites finally experienced peace after all the years of following everything else but the Lord.

When I read this passage, I asked God to help me understand what I was reading. He showed me that when Asa stepped in and directed the Israelites to the Lord, everything changed. Asa didn't do it just for himself; he led the people to do the same thing. In our own lives, when we turn from our wicked ways, we allow God to lead us in a new direction and remove the things that hinder us from experiencing His fullness.

In my life, this took years. Too many detours led me back to the place I started. I wandered in circles, repeating the same pattern I was familiar with, when I should've kept moving forward with my eyes on the Lord.

Second Chronicles 15:2–4 tells us,

> The LORD is with you when you are with him. If you seek him, he will be found by you, but if you abandon him, he will abandon you. For many years Israel has been without the true God, without a teaching priest, and without instruction, but when they turned to the LORD God of Israel in their distress and sought him, he was found by them.

I'm so thankful for Jesus and the Holy Spirit, and that They are never far away. When I've felt abandoned by God, it was because of me, not Him. That kind of sounds like something you'd say during a breakup: "It's not you, it's me. I'm just not ready for a relationship or a real commitment." But it was true. It was all me! When I chose to follow things that were not of God—or listen to the wrong people, or the enemy, or the lies in my own head over what God had spoken—that was when I wasn't walking in the fullness of God.

Today, I understand that there were times in my life when I was lukewarm. I don't want to be lukewarm. I don't want to just talk the talk. I want to live it. I don't want to be just delivered a little; I want to always be in reconstruction by the Lord's hand so I'm kept in good condition and operation.

I have experienced in the past being delivered "just a little" and still continuing in my own strength. Perhaps you have experienced this too. You have asked God into your heart and you were saved but you continued to live a life of trying to do what was right in your own strength. There are things that you have continued to struggle with, but you think it is too big for God to take it away, or you feel like you're not worthy enough for God to remove it, or you missed your chance. I want to tell you that nothing is too big for God and He never fails (see Matthew 19:26; Luke 1:37). Also, if God gave you a promise, He will fulfill it (see Hebrews 10:23). Seek Him, lay it at His feet, repent, and receive the deliverance He is longing to give! He can and will take it away. So many times we think we are waiting on the Lord, but I wonder if many times He is waiting on us. Waiting for us to open our heart, open our mouths, and say, "Lord, please forgive me and take away my iniquities" (see Psalm 51).

Don't settle for just a little deliverance. Take all your cares to the Lord and believe He can do mighty things—not just for you, but also for your family, your friends, and your enemies. Asa removed those foreign altars and sought the Lord, and "they" prospered (2 Chronicles 14:2–7). God can do the same for you and those around you.

## CHAPTER 13

# Out of the Wilderness

*In you our ancestors put their trust; they trusted you and you delivered them. To you they cried out and were saved; in you they trusted and were not put to shame.*

PSALM 22:4–5 NIV

Another part of the Journey song "Don't Stop Believin'" just came to my mind. You know, that part about people waiting up and down the boulevard and living just to find emotion. I don't know what your life has been like, but no matter your past, no matter the streets you've walked, no matter the things you've tried to run from, don't stop believing in God and what He has in store for your life. Pursue Him and the purpose He has for you.

I've shared my story so you can see what God has done in my life. Some of you may have your own story of pain and abuse. Maybe you fully relate to how I've felt. Maybe you've felt the freedom that only God gives but then ended up in the wilderness, not knowing how you got there. Maybe you're in the middle of a confusing or dark time right now. Maybe you're trying to hold on, but you're tired of fighting. Maybe you just feel numb—you've been hurt so bad that you just don't feel anymore.

No matter what place you're in right now, God can and will meet you. You're never too far from His reach. Jesus can heal and restore. Ephesians 3:20 tells us He can do so much more than we ask or imagine. Over the years, my mantra has been, "Have faith. Trust God. He is good. He is my joy. He loves me. He has the best in store for me." I've held on to the things He's promised me, even in the hardest times. I may have to remind myself of His promises, but I know God is faithful and I trust Him. I remember what Jesus did for me, who I am, and who I belong to.

Over the years, I've asked myself many questions as I've deepened my faith, and I want you to ask yourself the same ones. They've helped me as I've walked in faith, and I think they'll do the same for you.

- What do I believe about God, Jesus, the Holy Spirit, and the Bible?
- Who does God say I am?
- What is God's purpose for my life?
- Do I want the fullness of God? If not, why?
- Do I ever put God in a box? If so, how?
- How have I wandered in the wilderness like the Israelites?
- How have I listened to people over God? How can I stop doing that?
- Do I want freedom from the bondage that's kept me in prison for way too long? Why or why not?
- Do I believe God does miracles?
- What things have I put before God? How can I stop doing that?

- Do I trust God? Am I obedient?
- Do I think I'm unreachable?
- How have I surrendered my life to Him?
- Have I repented?
- What's holding me back from giving God my everything?

When we ask these questions and seek the answers in God's Word, in prayer, and in times of laying down each area of our life before God, that's when we experience the freedom and victory He has already won for us. He will come alongside us and uproot the sins of the past—those we've committed and those that have been committed against us. He is the Way, the Truth, and the Life (John 14:6), and the Light of the world who goes before us through the darkness.

One of my favorite Bible passages is Deuteronomy 30:1–11:

> When all these things happen to you—the blessings and curses I have set before you—and you *come to your senses* while you are in all the nations where the LORD your God has driven you, and you and your children *return to the LORD your God and obey him with all your heart and all your soul by doing everything I am commanding you* today, then he will restore your fortunes, have compassion on you, and gather you again from all the peoples where the LORD your God has scattered you. Even if your exiles are at the farthest horizon, he will gather you and bring you back from there. The LORD your God will bring you into the land your ancestors possessed, and you will take possession of it. He will cause you to prosper and multiply you more than he did your ancestors. The LORD your God will circumcise your heart and the hearts of your descendants, and you will love him with all your heart and all your soul so that you will live. The LORD your God will put all these curses on your enemies who hate and persecute you. Then

> you will again obey him and follow all his commands I am commanding you today. The LORD your God will make you prosper abundantly in all the work of your hands, your offspring, the offspring of your livestock, and the produce of your land. Indeed, the LORD will again delight in your prosperity, as he delighted in that of your ancestors, when you obey the LORD your God by keeping his commands and statutes that are written in this book of the law and return to him with all your heart and all your soul. This command that I give you today is certainly not too difficult or beyond your reach.

These verses talk about hope, but they also remind us of what will happen if we walk away from God. In the wilderness the Israelites went back and forth, turning to God and then back to idols. In Deuteronomy 30:16, God says, "For I'm commanding you today to love the LORD your God, to walk in his ways, and to keep his commands, statues and ordinances, so that you may live and multiply, and the LORD your God may bless you in the land you are entering to possess."

As I shared earlier, I was once like the Israelites, wandering around and around. God had me circle back around many times until I came to my senses. The path I've traveled is my journey; it's the road I had to take to get to the place I'm in now, although it may not have been the path I would've thought to choose or what I thought it should've looked like. Many of my decisions caused me more pain and suffering, just like the Israelites. They forgot what God took them out of, and when they chose to forget God and worship other things, they experienced what it was like to serve everything else but God.

I've done the same. I know what it's like to live for the Lord, to have the joy and peace that it brings, and I know what it's like to step away from that and endure the heartache and disaster that result. But I was able to turn back to God and keep moving forward. I won't stop because I want to end well, doing His will. That won't always be easy—Jesus told us that in this world we would have trouble (John 16:33)—but when I keep my eyes on Christ and walk with Him, I have calm in any storm I face.

> **I have calm in any storm I face.**

In Deuteronomy 31:8, Moses says, "The LORD is the one who will go before you. He will be with you; he will not leave you or abandon you. Do not be afraid or discouraged. Even in the wilderness God gave cover and provided." And in Deuteronomy 30:20, he says, "Love the LORD your God, obey him, and remain faithful to him. For he is your life, and he will prolong your days as you live in the land the Lord swore to give to your fathers Abraham, Isaac, and Jacob." What more can we ask for?

One day, as I was reading this passage in Deuteronomy, and another one in Joshua about the Israelites crossing over into the Promised Land, they showed me that it was when the Israelites stepped out of the wilderness, moving forward with their hearts set on God and not going backward to wander again, that the Israelites crossed over into what was promised to them.

I know storms will come and we can be knocked around, but if we keep moving forward, we won't have to go back to the wilderness. Returning to the wilderness is a choice. If we choose to walk in our old ways and remain in them, we'll find ourselves wandering around again. I don't want to be in that place again, and no doubt you don't either. Through our faithfulness, we keep moving forward—and into all that God has created us for. Joshua 1:9 (NIV) tells us, "Be strong and courageous. Do not be afraid; do not be discouraged, for the LORD your God will be with you wherever you go."

## CHAPTER 14

# Obedience Brings Fire

*Remain in me, as I remain in you. No branch can bear fruit by itself; it must remain in the vine. Neither can bear fruit unless you remain in me.*

**JOHN 15:4 NIV**

This chapter is something I originally wrote separate from this book. I had just gone on my third Freedom Women's Hike, which is three days and two nights of hiking on mountain trails. We carry forty-pound backpacks with everything we need and are disconnected from the outside world (no cell phones) so we can be free of distractions and experience what God wants us to experience.

Despite sleeping in a tent and enduring cold nights, aching legs, sore knees, and no bathrooms, every hike has been amazing in what God has done in and through these women on the mountain. This time, the day after the hike ended, I began to write about my experience, but that turned into me writing this book instead. I feel like it was my next step in leaving the wilderness.

In the last year, I've been in a place of obedience. That's not to say I'm living perfectly or my circumstances are perfect, because they aren't. I face battles daily, but I've been following through with the things God has shown me. Over the past few years, I thought I was doing pretty well, but then more recently God showed me that I needed to get serious about my obedience. In being bold for Him, speaking up when He guides me to, not hiding who I am in Him, and pointing others to Jesus, I've experienced the difference of what obedience to God looks and feels like. That's why I'm writing this book—I'm following through with what God has been leading me to do. And it doesn't just stop with me. What I've experienced isn't just for me. It's also for others.

*Obedience* can be defined as "compliance with an order, request, or law or submission to another authority" and "obedience to moral standards; obedience to conscience."[3] We all have a purpose, and when we take that first step of faith and receive Christ into our life, things begin to change. God had to do a *lot* of work in me. It took years for me to find healing.

God would drop special moments in my life, showing me things that He had for me and things He wanted me to do. He showed me that I was more than I let myself believe. I even became lukewarm in my faith. But I realized the danger of that and pursued Him, and He continued to lead me. When we begin to see the lies of the enemy, and we listen to God over everything else and choose obedience to the prompting of the Holy Spirit, we stop being lukewarm.

Obedience brings fire. No longer are we cold, no longer are we just warming up. We will swell with fire. We are the dried-up wood and God is the spark, and the resulting flame becomes a beautiful blaze that brings warmth to all those around it.

Every time I sit in front of a campfire, I want to get close enough to feel the warmth. I don't want anyone to stand in front of me and block the radiating heat. I don't want anyone to block my view of the flames. I love watching the movement of the fire and the glow of the embers as the wood crackles. The warmth and light bring me comfort, and I want to just sit and enjoy it. Then, when I leave the campfire, I can smell the smoke on my clothes and in my hair and it reminds me of the fire.

I believe that must have been what it was like to sit in the presence of Jesus. I wouldn't want anyone to block my view or keep me from seeing, hearing, and experiencing the fire He had within Him. His words and presence radiated to all who came in contact with Him, and I imagine that those who were touched by Him would've been like me when I leave a campfire and can still smell the smoke. When someone's truly been touched by Jesus, we can sense the difference in them. They've experienced the fire.

When we accept Christ, we have the Holy Spirit—the spark that ignites the fire within us. Even if our fire burns down to embers, those embers still produce heat. However, if we allow others or our experiences to remove our oxygen, then those embers eventually burn out. All hope isn't lost if that happens, though. With Christ nothing is lost. If we re-surrender our life to Him, that fire we thought was snuffed out will rise up in us once again. Unlike campfire embers that can't be ignited once they've gone out, the embers of our life can be brought back to life with the breath of God.

When we walk in obedience to God's Word and His promptings in our life, we experience more and more of His power. When we trust God so much that we let Him lead in every area of our life, that's when we stand firm when things come against us. We keep our eyes on God's purpose for our life. We submit to the Holy Spirit, who will flow freely in our life and around those we come in contact with so they too will experience the freedom and purpose that God has for them.

In my obedience, I hear God more clearly and can act upon His requests more quickly. In my obedience and trust of Him in everything, God expects me to do what He asks. It still blows my mind that God would trust me in this way. I used to tell God, "I don't trust myself, but, God, I trust you." I said that to Him over and over, and one day He revealed to me that He trusted me. I'm still in awe of that moment because I've messed up so many times and couldn't imagine God trusting me.

> **In my obedience, I hear God more clearly...**

God trusted Moses and Abraham and others to do what He asked of them. Even in their weaknesses, they were obedient. We now benefit from their faith and obedience like so many before us. I'm not Moses and I'm not Abraham, but I serve the same God. I talk to the same God, I cry out to the same God, and I listen to the same God. This also blows my mind. The God of Moses and Abraham is the God we serve today.

I like to think about trust in the context of children. We don't trust children with everything from the time they're born. They need to learn and grow and mature. The first time I let Faith stay home alone, I'd waited until she was a certain age, and then I gave her some rules ("Don't use the stove or oven, don't open the door to anyone even if you know them, and make sure you do your homework"). I also left her alone for only a short amount of time. I wanted to make sure she could follow my directions before I'd allow her to do it again. I needed to make sure I could trust her with the things I asked of her. When she followed through and obeyed, I trusted her.

God does the same with us. He will test us to see how we do. Sometimes we can be trusted in certain areas but not in others. It took me a long time to obey enough to be trusted, and I went around and around because I didn't get it the first time—or sometimes the second or third time. I'm thankful God is faithful and didn't give up on me. Romans 12:2 (NIV) says, "Do not conform to the pattern of this world, but be transformed by the renewing of the mind. Then you will be able to test and approve what God's will is—his good, pleasing and perfect will."

My story and your story may not be in the Scriptures, but all those who have accepted Christ as their Savior have their names written in heaven and the Book of Life (Luke 10:20; Philippians 4:3). The Bible is God's spoken words filled with promises and glimpses of who God is and who we are. In Christ we are everything we were created for. With Him, we lack nothing. Without Him, we are lost.

Remember how, in the introduction, I was wondering what made my life special enough that I should write a book, and the answer I received was, Nothing—yet everything? The nothing is because I'm nothing without Christ, and the everything is because I'm everything in Him.

From the moment I was conceived I was not destroyed. Though Satan and his entourage lurked around and played a hand in my life, I was still not destroyed. I can say, as Joseph did in Genesis 50:20, "You intended to harm me, but God intended it for good to accomplish what is now being done, the saving of many lives."

Satan also went after Christ. He used people to go after Him even as an infant (Matthew 2:16), and he confronted Jesus in the wilderness (Mathew 4; Luke 4) after He was baptized by John the Baptist in the Jordan. Jesus was full of the Holy Spirit, who led Him into the wilderness (Judean Desert) for forty days and forty nights, where He fasted and prayed. Satan tried to tempt Jesus and even used Scripture to try to manipulate Him.

When I'm hungry and physically weak, it's easy to distract me and I may not react in the proper way. But Jesus was full of the Holy Spirit. He was prepared because He knew the truth and He knew the ways of His Father. So, yes, Jesus was no doubt hungry, tired, thirsty, and weak physically, but that didn't stop Him from speaking the truth back to Satan. Each time Satan tried to manipulate Jesus, Jesus came back with the word of truth and shut him down each time. Jesus was obedient in His response.

The third time Jesus replied, "Go away, Satan! For it is written: Worship the Lord your God, and serve only him" (Matthew 4:10). And you know what Satan did? He left. You know why? Because of the power of Christ. And when we are saved and filled with the Holy Spirit, we carry the power of Christ in us. We have the power through Christ to say, "Go away, Satan!" We speak the truth and he must flee! When Satan left, angels came and served Jesus (v. 11). How great is our God, that He will send angels down to serve us.

Jesus spent forty days and forty nights, not years, in the wilderness. I laugh sometimes because I thought, *Well, if I was more like Jesus, I wouldn't have had to wander as long as I did—if I had spent that time in prayer and fasting and being prepared to speak against the lies.* But my path is what brought me to the place I am now—a place of obedience and allowing God to speak against the lies and manipulation of my past. I'm not forgotten or forsaken, I'm not abandoned or worthless. I am everything in Christ, and this is true for all who believe.

You, too, can speak up and refuse to be destroyed. You, too, can allow God to uproot the things that no longer belong in your life and allow His healing power to restore you and be the living water that brings root to a new seed.

> **Speak up and refused to be destroyed.**

## CHAPTER 15

# A New Life

*It is for freedom that Christ has set us free. Stand firm, then, and do not let yourselves be burdened again by a yoke of slavery.*

**GALATIANS 5:1 NIV**

God has healed my past, and I now see how everything I've experienced, good and bad, has made me who I am and molded me into what God needs me to be. I've tried to put God in a box way too many times, like He had limits and couldn't do the impossible. When I step out of the way and allow Him to do what only He can, I see and experience the power of Christ. To surrender to His will has brought freedom and peace, and it's helped me to have compassion for and to forgive others. I want others to walk in freedom as well. I want them to experience the power of Christ in their life.

My prayer and hope for you as you've read what I've shared is that it opens the door for God to speak into the areas of your life that may have been hidden from others, and from God. Yes, God already knows, but many times we push things back and make believe it doesn't have a hold on us, but in reality it will surface at times. God has given us free will to make that choice to follow Him. In return He saves us and gives us a new life in Him.

John 3:16 (NIV) says, "For God so loved the world the he gave his one and only Son, that whoever believes in him shall not perish but have eternal life." Before Christ, people had to sacrifice animals for their sins, but when Christ came, He was an example who taught us how to live. He gave us wisdom from God and became our sacrifice, our salvation for our sins. We couldn't do it on our own. Galatians 1:4 (NIV) says Jesus is the one "who gave himself for our sins to rescue us from the present evil age, according to the will of our God and Father." Jesus died on the cross for us and rose three days later (Luke 24:6–7; Mark 16:5–7). Jesus was not destroyed; He was fulfilling the promise of His Father (see 1 Corinthians 15:4). Satan thought he won that day, but God used Jesus to reconcile us back to Him. Through Him we could turn from our wicked ways and be free from the slavery of sin.

My questions now are, Do you believe in God? Have you asked Christ to be your Savior? Christ came to die for our sins. His doing so was the beginning of a new way of life and an opening of the door to freedom. Romans 10:9–10 says, "If you confess with your mouth, 'Jesus is Lord,' and believe in your heart that God raised him from the dead, you will be saved. One believes with the heart, resulting in righteousness, and one confesses with the mouth, resulting in salvation." If you haven't made Jesus your Savior and Lord, and you want to now, pray and ask Him into your heart. Acts 2:21 (ASV) says, "Whoever shall call on the name of the Lord shall be saved." Begin this new journey with the Lord and allow Him to walk alongside you as you walk the path of life.

I asked Jesus to be my Savior when I was a child. Then I said the prayer a few times later in my life as if it didn't work the first time and I needed to be saved again. I believed that Jesus saved me the first time I asked, but it took me years before I made Him my Lord and allowed Him to take control of my life. There were a lot of thoughts and ideas in my head that needed to be removed to make room for God's thoughts. I needed sanctification.

Sanctification means to be set apart. I love how billygrahamlibrary.org explains it:

> By definition, sanctification means to be reserved for holy use. The objective of every believer should be to hastily pursue this. Sanctification demonstrates the urgency to be emptied out of anything that impairs against being a useful vessel for God's glory. It's a process that starts in the heart and transforms outward living. The Bible is the instrument that God uses to clean our hearts.[4]

First John 17:17 (NIV) says, "Sanctify them in the truth; your word is truth." And 1 Thessalonians 5:23 (NKJV) says, "Now may the God of peace Himself sanctify you completely; and may your whole spirit, soul, and body be preserved blameless at the coming of our Lord Jesus Christ."

My hope and prayer for you is that you begin to open up to a God who can do the impossible and that no matter where you are in life at this moment He will meet you right here, right now! No matter whether you're in a place of just beginning to open up and want to be healed, or you're starting a new relationship with Christ, or you've already made that decision to follow Christ but you feel like you're in the wilderness or in a storm, or you're still living in the past, or you're wondering what your purpose is, Christ is right here ready and waiting to walk with you in every area of your life.

Lord, I pray that each person who reads your words in this book is forever changed. That they receive your word as truth. That they begin to soak in who you are, who they are, and who you have called them to be. That they find freedom in every area of their life. That the sins of the past will be uprooted and will no longer have power or control over them anymore. Lord, speak to their mind, heart, and spirit, and draw them into an intimate relationship with You. I thank You, Lord, for what You are already doing in each person. In Your name, Jesus, amen.

# APPENDIX

# The Effects of Childhood Abuse

I have learned some things about abuse over the years, but when I began to write about my past is when I decided to look up current information on the effects of abuse during childhood. A friend who is a therapist gave me a list of resources, and one was the Child Welfare Information Gateway, which is described as "a service of the Children's Bureau, Administration for Children and Families, U.S. Department of Health and Human Services." Here is some of the information I found while looking through their sources.

Child abuse during infancy and early childhood can cause disruptions in brain/cognitive development, social and emotional development, and academic achievement. A big part of brain structure is shaped from birth to age three, and the first eight years of life build a foundation for future learning, health, and life stresses.[6]

Adverse fetal and early childhood experiences can lead to physical and chemical disruptions in the brain that can last a lifetime and cause issues with future learning capacity, behavior, and physical and mental health outcomes. Genetics certainly play a role, but a child's environment can alter family inheritance. Children are typically born with the capacity to learn to control impulses, focus attention, and absorb their experiences as early as the first year of life. When environmental abuse and/or neglect happen, this development can be disrupted.[7]

When a study was conducted on the brains of children who had been abused and children who had not, they found the children who'd been abused had

- Decreased size of the corpus callous, which is the area of cortical functioning, motor, sensory, and cognitive motor skills.
- Decreased size of the hippocampus, which is the area responsible for learning and memory
- Dysfunction in the HPA (hypothalamic-pituitary-adrenal) axis, which is the area responsible for stress response
- Less volume in the prefrontal cortex, which is the area responsible for behavior, emotional balance, and perception
- Overaction in the amygdala, which is the area responsible for processing emotions and determining reactions to potentially stressful or dangerous situations
- Reduced volume of the cerebellum, which affects motor skills and coordination[8]

Emotional abuse and neglect during childhood can result in permanent changes in the development of the brain, and these changes can cause future issues even into adulthood, such as behavioral, emotional, and social-functioning challenges. They can also lead to a higher risk for substance abuse and developing mental health issues such as anxiety, bipolar disorder, depression, personality disorders, and psychosis. Some people may struggle with feelings of being on alert or unable to relax, fearfulness, learning deficiencies, social challenges, feelings of hopelessness, low self-esteem, automatic negative thoughts, and stress coping problems.[9]

With sexual abuse, 91 percent of abusers are someone the victim knows, and often the victim does not report the abuse out of fear or shame.[10] (This resonated with me since it was my story exactly.)

People who've been sexually abused can respond in different ways. Some will relive events through flashbacks or memories, while others will have no memory of the abuse. Some will avoid intimacy or sexual relationships, while others will engage in unhealthy sexual practices. Feeling numbness, fear, or shame is common. Dissociation (having no memory of the abuse) is a natural defense mechanism where the brain tries to protect the person from painful memories. Victims of sexual abuse may also get startled easily, develop obsessive compulsive disorder, have difficulty sleeping or sleep too much, have difficulty concentrating, develop eating disorders, or have a higher risk of future abuse. They can also struggle with heightened awareness/fear of danger, trust issues, fear of intimacy, and relationship instability.[11]

Abuse can also cause long-term consequences such as a higher risk for future health problems like diabetes, arthritis, high blood pressure, brain damage, migraines, cancer, stroke, bowel disease, and chronic fatigue syndrome. There is also a higher risk of alcohol and drug abuse, adult criminality, and future abuse.[12]

The human mind is complex, and there's still so much to be learned about it. The definition of mind is "the element of a person that enables them to be aware of the world and their experiences."[13] Our mind allows us to think, to feel, to perceive, to will, and to reason. It's the faculty of consciousness, thought, intention, desire, recollection, and memory. Therefore it also affects our disposition and mood.

The effects of abuse can distort how we think, feel, and act; our intentions; our desires; our views; our moods; and more. I struggled with unhealthy ways of thinking and feeling. I doubt I even thought about the word unhealthy in that context. I was just trying to survive in my thoughts and not breakdown emotionally. For a long time, I didn't understand that I needed a different way of thinking. Blocking things out was my way of coping, but that isn't healthy.

The Bible also talks about the mind and how important it is. Here are some verses that talk about the mind and have helped me refocus and put my mind back on Christ:

- We are to have the mind of Christ (1 Corinthians 2:16).
- We are to have the same mindset as Christ (Philippians 2:5).
- We are to have minds that are alert and fully sober (1 Peter 1:13).
- We are to set our mind on things above, not on earthly things (Colossians 3:2).
- We are to take every thought captive (2 Corinthians 10:3–5).
- We are to be transformed by a renewal of our mind (Romans 12:2).
- The mind governed by the spirit is life and peace (Romans 8:6).

I shared earlier in this book about one thing that I learned that stuck with me and that I have to apply daily in my life and that is "we can't always control the thoughts that come to our mind, but we can choose to replace them." Allow Gods word to transform you by the renewal of your mind. I hope you begin to recognize the lies, the distractions, the wrong way of thinking that you experience and say "no more" and replace them with the goodness of God! You are unique and wonderfully made and loved by a glorious God!

# NOTES

## CHAPTER 8: OUT WITH THE OLD

1. "How to Keep Clothes Smelling Fresh in Drawers, Storage, and Closets," April 13, 2022, https://www.closetamerica.com/article/how-to-keep-clothes-smelling-fresh-in-drawers-storage-and-closets/.

2. Oxford Languages Dictionary, s.v. "condemned," https://www.oxfordlearnersdictionaries.com/us/definition/american_english/condemn#:~:text=condemn%20somebody%2Fsomething%20(for%2F,was%20condemned%20as%20lacking%20integrity.

## CHAPTER 14: OBEDIENCE BRINGS FIRE

3. Oxford Languages Dictionary, s.v. "obedience," https://www.oxfordlearnersdictionaries.com/us/definition/english/obedience?q=obedience.

## CHAPTER 15: A NEW LIFE

4. "5 Things the Bible Says about Sanctification," The Billy Graham Library, March 5, 2021, https://billygrahamlibrary.org/blog-5-things-the-bible-says-about-sanctification/.

## APPENDIX: THE EFFECTS OF CHILDHOOD ABUSE

5. "Child Welfare Information Gateway Unveils New Website," Administration for Children and Families, https://www.acf.hhs.gov/archive/blog/2014/12/child-welfare-information-gateway-unveils-new-website.

6. "Child Welfare Information Gateway Unveils New Website," Administration for Children and Families, https://www.acf.hhs.gov/archive/blog/2014/12/child-welfare-information-gateway-unveils-new-website.

7. "Child Welfare Information Gateway Unveils New Website," Administration for Children and Families, https://www.acf.hhs.gov/archive/blog/2014/12/child-welfare-information-gateway-unveils-new-website.

8. verywellminded.com.

9. Helplingsurvivors.org.

10. helpingsurvivors.org.

11. helpingsurvivors.org.

12. helpingsurvivors.org.

13. Oxford Languages Dictionary, s.v. "mind," https://www.oxfordlearnersdictionaries.com/us/definition/english/mind_1?q=mind.

## 🌿 JOHN 15:1-5 NIV 🌿

""I am the true vine, and my Father is the gardener. He cuts off every branch in me that bears no fruit, while every branch that does bear fruit he prunes so that it will be even more fruitful. You are already clean because of the word I have spoken to you. Remain in me, as I also remain in you. No branch can bear fruit by itself; it must remain in the vine. Neither can you bear fruit unless you remain in me. "I am the vine; you are the branches. If you remain in me and I in you, you will bear much fruit; apart from me you can do nothing."

NOT DESTROYED